Praise for *Happiness Beyond Thought: A Practical Guide to Awakening*

"Husband, father, scientist, military officer, and senior executive in industry and academia, Gary Weber has led a full and successful worldly life. Throughout all of this, Gary has relentlessly pursued a path of practice and inquiry in order to understand life and achieve enlightenment. It is rare to find one who has reached this goal, and rarer still to find such a one who has been so immersed in worldly life.

With this book, Gary has successfully integrated his profound realization with traditional non-dualistic teachings, as well as insights from Zen Buddhism and modern brain research, into a practical path that uses Yoga's time-tested practices of asana, pranayama, chanting and meditation to illumine a path to enlightenment for the modern reader."

Gary Kraftsow, author of *Yoga for Wellness* and *Yoga for Transformation*

"Gary Weber offers a treasure chest of practices for the serious practitioner seeking liberation. On your own journey towards awakening, savor these simple, easy to follow practices culled from Weber's study with his primary teacher Ramana Maharshi, his on-going exploration of Zen meditation practice, and the life-enhancing results of his experiments on the laboratory floor of his yoga mat."

Amy Weintraub, author of *Yoga for Depression*

"I've had the wonderful privilege of experiencing Gary in action over many years both as friend and teacher. Gary is the rare gem who points directly to what we really are at the heart of our being—timeless Presence—ever-present Stillness that is always immediately available; yet which we fail to recognize because of our over-identification with the changing circumstances of our lives. Gary offers us a fresh view, based on his firsthand experience of the paradox of enlightenment: that while there is nothing we can ultimately do to awaken to our timeless Presence, there are exquisite perennial practices of 'non-doing' that prepare the ground and clear the way for awakening. Gary beckons us to awaken from our dream of separation and realize our timeless and non-separate oneness with everything. Few may take up his call, but no pointer is more needed than his to call for us to come home."

Richard Miller, PhD author of *Yoga Nidra: The Meditative Heart of Yoga*

"If you're interested in understanding the many levels of spiritual reality, or the secrets uncovered in a cave in the Himalayas, or what adventures lie in store for you after you die, then Gary Weber's book is definitely not for you. There's no metaphysical speculation here, no religiosity, and no mystification. Instead, as its title points out, this is a *practical* guide. It's as close as they come to a "How To" manual, not only for getting enlightened, but also for what to expect when you're there."

James Lough, Ph.D., Editor of *Sites of Insight: A Guide to Colorado Sacred Places*

HAPPINESS
Beyond Thought

HAPPINESS
Beyond Thought

A Practical Guide to Awakening

Gary Weber, Ph. D.

iUniverse, Inc.

New York Lincoln Shanghai

Happiness Beyond Thought
A Practical Guide to Awakening

iUniverse books may be ordered through booksellers or by contacting:

iUniverse
2021 Pine Lake Road, Suite 100
Lincoln, NE 68512
www.iuniverse.com
1-800-Authors (1-800-288-4677)

You should not undertake any exercise regimen recommended in this book before consulting your personal physician. Neither the author nor the publisher shall be responsible or liable for any loss or damage allegedly arising as a consequence of your use or application of any information or suggestions contained in this book.

ISBN-13: 978-0-595-41856-5 (pbk)
ISBN-13: 978-0-595-86201-6 (ebk)
ISBN-10: 0-595-41856-2 (pbk)
ISBN-10: 0-595-86201-2 (ebk)

Printed in the United States of America

Dedicated to Ramana Maharshi who found me lost and wandering in a dark forest, taught me what inquiry, love, and surrender were and brought nobody home

Acknowledgements

My deepest appreciation for the kindness of Sri V. S. Ramanan, President of Sri Ramanasramam (Ramana Maharshi's ashram in Tiruvannamalai, South India) for his permission to use Ramana's teachings and photograph, without which this book could not have taken shape.

I would also like to extend my thanks to Russill Paul for permission to draw from his work on Vedic chanting and chant arrangements and to David Godman for permission to quote from his book on Annamalai Swami.

My deep gratitude for the many hours and years I have shared with so many wonderful teachers and fellow travelers. Although too numerous to mention, those who had particular impact were Toni Packer, Roshi Eido Shimano, J. Krishnamurti, Swami Rama, Amrit Desai, Adyashanti, Gangaji, Poonjaji, Swami Chetanananda, Swami Viditatmananda and of course my Sat Guru, Ramana Maharshi. No words would ever be enough.

A special thanks to Gary Kraftsow and Richard Miller. I spent much time with each of them over many years as friend and fellow spiritual traveler.

Thanks to those who read, commented on, and dramatically improved the manuscript over its long inception, particularly James Lough, Richard Miller, Amy Weintraub, Gary Kraftsow, Stephan Bodian, Joan Ruvinsky, my daughter Paige, and last, but far from least, my wife, Jeanne. Thanks to Ralph Moon for assistance with the translation of Nirvana Shatakam.

I give many thanks for/to "my students." They are the voice of the Universe asking itself questions to which it already knows the answers, yet it still finds delight in the beautiful mysterious dance.

A majority of any author profits from this book will be donated to support work with disabled children in southern India.

The author can be contacted at non_dual_awakening@earthlink.net.

Contents

Introduction

"A veil was lifted. All of a sudden there was recognition that I'm not my thoughts. Everyone always says it but I never felt it. It turns out I'm actually not the voice in my "head" that says stuff. That's separate from me. Immediately after was the recognition "I am awareness" ... I really am ad hoc. Thoughts occur, feelings occur, body occurs (physical sensations), I witness.... It's so big, though, the feel. I am AWARENESS, not just I am aware. That's big ... Better: awareness is aware.... it's less personal than me.... and regardless of what I want, what is is and what will happen will happen."

This e-mail from a student of mine captures what awakening is. It is the clear recognition that we aren't our thoughts or the stories that we tell ourselves. We aren't the bodies that we worry about so much. We aren't the sensations that we crave and fear. We are the already present happiness, the still awareness beyond thought within which all of this occurs. That awareness is beyond fear, beyond suffering, beyond death itself.

This book offers a direct practical approach to having that recognition unfold. It uses practices from yoga, Zen meditation, and Eastern philosophies in a synergistic, holistic way. Although these practices are powerful by themselves, the odds of your awakening increase significantly through using them together. You can do these practices, as I did, while living a full, active, engaged life in today's world including working and having a family. You don't need to retire to a cave, change your name, leave your family, stop working, change your hairdo, go to India, or get a new wardrobe. You do not need to surrender your money and possessions to some colorfully-dressed and impressively-titled keepers of secret knowledge and practices.

The best news of all is that the truth of who you really are isn't outside you nor is it some experience that you have to struggle to replicate. Your ultimate reality, your enlightened state, is already pre-installed. You come right from the factory with the software already downloaded and running. All that you have to do is to understand what is blocking you from seeing it and to realize that it has always been there. With that, you will see that it is what you are.

The direct approach to awakening into the happiness that you already are is not to gather more knowledge or experiences, but to recognize and remove the residue from the ones that you have already had. A helpful metaphor can be one from the ancient Egyptians.

Scales of Judgment

This image depicts the scales of judgment that the Egyptians believed were used to measure one's worthiness to go to their equivalent of heaven. The recently deceased folk would go to the underworld and be led to these scales. On the left side would be placed the deceased's heart; a feather was placed on the right side. If the deceased's heart was heavier than a feather, a ferocious demon immediately devoured the heart and the folk. If the heart was lighter than a feather, eternal bliss and happiness followed.

We will go through many approaches in this work, all with the purpose of (en)lightening your heart by clearing away the confusion, conditioning and thought that hide your natural reality. We will not be adding yet more knowledge and confusion which would only make your metaphorical heart heavier. We will draw upon yoga, Zen meditation and Eastern philosophy in this lightening operation.

Traditional yoga as normally practiced now in the West with its focus on achieving certain postures (asanas) and bodily perfection naturally leads to comparisons and conflicts. Very few yoga classes involve any type of meditation or meaningful investigation of mind or consciousness. Even fewer courses offer any insight into what is really achievable through yoga beyond a few catch phrases or even how to use asanas for awakening from the dream that we are.

In a typical course, an ad hoc practitioner of yoga is created who is subsequently enhanced, measured and critiqued; this does not lead to a lightened heart. What results is more confusion and anxiety and yet another new troubled and complex persona. This is a step backwards, even if the practices are elegant and esoteric and lead to fascinating party conversation with new and interesting people and special clothes and gear. I say this as someone who has done well over 10,000 hours of asanas in over 35 years of practice with many different teachers in many different schools.

Zen meditation is focused on meditation techniques, often in a highly-structured format intended to produce awakening/enlightenment. However, what more often results is a doer with nifty badges, names, clothes and titles who has learned many elegant practices. The result can be a disciplined and focused mind, some temporary relief of stress, possibly intermittent stopping of thoughts and some passing spiritual experiences. What seldom results is a transformation in consciousness so that you become your natural state of stillness and happiness.

Most meditation practices also do not incorporate a physical practice done with much understanding. Without this, there is little possibility of activating and addressing deeply-held conditioning, memories or fears that may be locked in your physiological structure. This is a great opportunity missed as the body knows on a cellular level the real truth that we are.

These comments arise from a meditation practice that has spanned over three decades and over 13,000 hours with several of the best known teachers, Zen and otherwise, including being passed on the level of understanding.

Eastern philosophies, including Hindu, Buddhist, Taoist and Sufi approaches, are sophisticated and elegant. They can provide, particularly for the Western mind, powerful new tools to deconstruct or reconstruct the heavily-conditioned mind into a more holistic model and potentially even to transcend it completely. Unfortunately, what often results is yet another religion with rigidified beliefs, certainties and practices far from the understanding of its founder(s). It does, however, provide many opportunities for new, exciting and endless philosophical discussions. Philosophy can be a great ally on the path to awakening, but it can be a terrible master.

In this book, many different practices will be presented that draw upon the strengths of these approaches. They will be merged in a constructive and practical way. The focus will be on using them to produce a deep questioning of the nature, structure and functioning of the mind and the ego/I. Doing this questioning with a strong desire for the truth can result in a deep understanding which weakens the hold of thoughts and the I. This can open the way to realizing the already existing happiness that you naturally are that is there beyond the operation of thought.

Most languages are constructed around a subject who does something with an object. We call that subject "I". You can ultimately discover that the "I" is not real. However, it is virtually impossible to find something to put in its place linguistically that will not be hard to understand, clumsy and obtuse. Different approaches like using the third person, substituting a lower case "i", trying not to use a subject, writing in some passive voice, etc. were all tried. They were universally rejected by readers, editors, and reviewers. So an "I" will be used in this book, even though it is fictitious, in the interest of readability. There are some aboriginal tongues that supposedly don't have a subject, but since neither you nor I know them, we will have to make do with English as it is. It will be kind of like knowing that the Thames River in London is pronounced "temz". It'll just be our little secret.

There will be much discussion of non-duality, also known as "advaita" in Sanskrit from "a"—not and "dvaita"—two. These terms simply mean that everything is really one thing even though it appears to be a bunch of subjects and objects. It also logically follows that you, as a separate entity, don't exist in the way that you think you do. It is a "bad news, good news" story; the bad news is that you don't exist (actually it isn't that bad), the good news is that you're everything. Not a bad trade.

We will start with some simple exercises to look at the nature of thought, how it functions and what our (mis)conceptions are of mind and thought. You will see chapters in the Practice section dedicated to utilizing yogic approaches like postures (asanas), breathing (pranayama), and chanting for awakening. There are even a few words on diet and chakras. There are also chapters focused on Self realization through meditation, inquiry, the use of affirmations and negations, and surrender, one of the most misunderstood topics.

The Text section draws upon three of the most powerful texts for awakening. One is about 80 years old, another 1200 years old, and the third approximately 2500 years old. Each text is given in the Sanskrit in which it was written. It is then translated, explained and commented on, perhaps with a poem. It is not necessary to learn the Sanskrit. You will not be more enlightened if you learn the Sanskrit version. It will appeal to some; others will avoid it like the plague like I did, originally.

All of these texts and practices have been used in classes or workshops with real folk just like you. The format throughout is questions and answers as that was most effective and useful in my personal practice and in working with others.

There is nothing here that is beyond you. It is hopefully as practical, simple and natural as it can be, as is awakening itself.

It is not intended that you will do every practice or study every text in the order presented or even at all. Some will catch your interest immediately, others will be of no interest whatsoever at the present time, or perhaps ever. As you go through the book, the practices and lines of text that are yours will grab you and hold you—go with them as far as they take you. When they have lost their hold, they have done their job and it is time for you to move on to another. Once the boat has taken you across the river, leave it on the bank. Don't keep trying to make it work again just because it worked before.

You may have heard that you are already enlightened and perfect and that there is nothing that you need to do. You may have also read that there is no you and that everything is beyond your control, so doing a practice is impossible. However, if just hearing those statements were enough, you and the millions who have heard them would already be enjoying endless uncaused stillness and peace. If you are, you don't need this book. If that isn't your reality, you will need to do some work. This book, which has come from nowhere and is written by no one, will give you approaches that can make that realization yours and the ever present mysterious reality and happiness that you are apparent. Let's get to it.

Practices

A. Some exercises for understanding your mind and thoughts

Let's begin by seeing what the nature of thought is and how it functions through doing some simple exercises. If you are going to move beyond thought, you at least need to understand the type of challenge that you face.

A helpful approach is to investigate the I as if it was applying for a job, realizing of course that you are both the interviewer and the applicant. What are your expectations that the I needs to fulfill it is it to be successful in this job? Typical workshop lists when I have asked this include "protect me from harm", "make good choices", "remember what is important", "be there only when needed", "remember only good experiences", "don't obsess about the past", "make me happy", "know what's going to happen to me", etc. As you work your way through the exercises which follow, see if the I in which so much is invested is capable of delivering on these expectations and what an I actually is.

Several different approaches to this much misunderstood, but omnipresent topic of thought can be helpful. Drawing a few insights, which may surprise you, from Ramana Maharshi's *Upadesa Saram* discussed in more detail in the Texts section:

17. If you search for your mind, you will find that it doesn't exist.

8. Instead of meditating on an object, know that you are That, the One.

19. See where the I comes from and it will disappear.

Using this guidance, let's first explore the nature of our minds.

What types of thoughts do you have?

First, focus on the types of thoughts that you have. Sitting quietly, watch the breath until it becomes slower and calmer so that separate thoughts or short thought streams on one subject can be identified. Begin placing thoughts into three buckets. If thoughts were real, you could use external buckets, but since thoughts are not real, you will have to make do with internal buckets, which are also only thoughts.

The first bucket is for thoughts about the past: pains, pleasures, regrets, joys, "shudas," "cudas," etc. The second bucket is filled with thoughts about the present: what is NOW, right this instant. The third bucket is filled with thoughts about the future: plans, fantasies, fears of failures or pains, hoped for successes and pleasures, "I'm going to tell her when I see her," etc.

Do not count sensations without thoughts, characterization or classification attached to them. These are the present. If a sensation is followed by recognition, naming, categorization, analysis, memory, and a story or something to be done about it, that's not NOW. The pure sensation is gone and thought has arrived on the scene with an experiencer, or a doer who is going to do something about it.

For example, if you hear a car passing it can be just sound, just the pure sound being received by an open, clear and aware receptor-hearing without a hearer or something that is heard. If the sound becomes a car, then a car outside, then a car outside making too much noise, then a car outside making too much noise that someone needs to do something about, then that isn't in the present.

Fill your buckets for about 5 minutes. At the end of five minutes, look at your buckets and see what has happened. Which of the buckets shown in the graphic below are full, or nearly full, for you? Are any buckets virtually empty? What does this tell you about your thoughts?

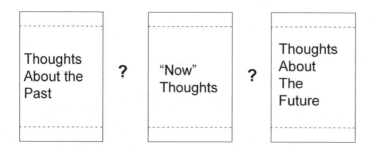

What is the distribution of thoughts between the past, present and future?

Most folk spend virtually all of their lives in their thoughts, in the past and future. You are almost never in the mystery and wonder of what is really unfolding just as it is, NOW. When you are eating, you are thinking about work. When you are at work, you are dreaming of seeing your friends at a party. When you are at the party with your friends, you are thinking about talking to someone else, what you're going to say next, what you just said that was wrong or brilliant, or being at a better party.

Recognizing that you live a second-hand life can be an important realization. Seeing that thoughts rob you of your life, of your inherent happiness and awareness can open the way to letting go of them. Can you see that this fascination and fixation with your thoughts means that you are always somewhere else in some other time? Why are you afraid to be here, in this present, right NOW? Don't let your life be like the John Lennon quote, "what happens to you while you're making other plans."

What is the path of your thinking? Do your thought streams follow a pattern?

Sitting still and quiet, with a piece of paper and something to write with, trace the flow of your thought streams. As a stream of thoughts about one topic starts, draw a straight line and continue with that line until another thought stream on another topic takes over and interrupts the first. With this shift, draw the line in another direction until that thought stream is interrupted by another. Continue for three to five minutes.

What was your experience? Is your thinking a long, continuous stream of thoughts about one topic, or is it random, even chaotic, with many short streams on many unrelated topics? Which of the patterns shown below was most like yours? Were your surprised at the outcome?

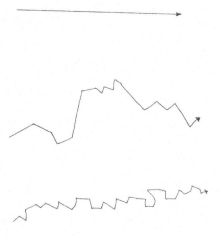

As many times as I have done this in workshops and classes, no one has ever drawn a straight line; most draw something like the bottom line. Folk are surprised by this outcome. They can't believe that is how it really is. We like to believe that our thoughts are some continuous sequence of rational considerations and conclusions that we control. Is that what your thoughts are? Are you in control of your thinking process? Are you making the decisions to start the next stream of thoughts and which subject will be next? Is this process in control or out of control? If you believe your thoughts are who you are, what does this tell you? Who's driving this bus?

How often is "I, me, mine" part of a thought?

From a centered, calm, still space, mentally construct two new buckets into which you will place your thoughts. It may be helpful to go back to your breath for several minutes and focus on your exhales and inhales before beginning. The first bucket will contain those thoughts that have an "I," "me," or "my" in them. The "I," "me," "my," may be explicit or implied, obvious or slightly hidden somewhere. The second bucket will have those thoughts that do not have an "I," "me," or "my" in them.

At the end of five minutes, see what is in the two buckets. Which of the situations depicted in the graphic below applies to what you found? Did you have many thoughts that didn't have an "I" or its sisters somewhere in them?

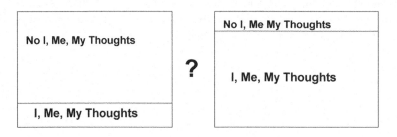

Do Most Thoughts Contain An I, Me or Mine?

Is this what you expected?

Most people find that most of their thoughts, perhaps all of them, contain the "I" in some manifestation. This conclusion that virtually all thoughts contain the

I is also a surprise. It really is "all about you". We would like to believe that our thoughts are about everyone else, the world's problems, the cure for cancer, etc., when it is actually always about us. Even when you do appear to care about someone else, if you look and feel carefully, you will see that it is really about you. You are really interested in feeling or being seen as some idealized version of yourself, perhaps one that is a better, improved version, a good person, rather than what you sometimes feel you are.

The good news in that this discovery provides a window into awakening. If you realize clearly that thoughts are robbing you of your happiness and your "I" is the root of most of your thoughts, you can find for a way forward. This forms the rationale for the inquiry into the nature of the "I" as the most direct and certain way to be free from the tyranny of thoughts. It is, even for those who have been on the spiritual path for a long time, the often overlooked key. It is much more exciting to be someone looking everywhere for the answer, reading, practicing, traveling to exotic locations and discussing it with fellow travelers, than it is to turn the quest around and inquire as to who, or what it is that is the real problem.

Can you sit still and do nothing?

Find a quiet, comfortable place where you will have some time without any immediate obligations of concerns. This exercise is very simple. Just stop everything and sit still and do nothing for at least an hour, preferably longer.

What happens? Are you able to be still and quiet and yet aware and attentive, or are you uneasy, nervous, and anxious, bored, wanting to do something, anything? Why is doing nothing such a difficult place to be? Who is it that has this need to be doing something?

Can you be aware of a doer arising, sometimes feverishly trying to find something to do? Can you see fear arising? What is there to be afraid of? You are in a comfortable, quiet place, with no immediate demands that need to be dealt with. Why is there this anxiety, this fear of not doing something?

Are you afraid of becoming nothing if you aren't doing something? Are you afraid of the emptiness that might arise if you are doing nothing? Who is it that has this fear of the emptiness, of the nothingness, or of perhaps not existing?

There are many different techniques and practices in Zen meditation. One of them is called "shikan taza". It is regarded as one of the most demanding practices and is normally only given to more advanced practitioners. Some schools don't even use it. The guidance given with this practice is that it typically cannot be done for more than half an hour as it is too demanding for the mind. What is this practice? "Shikan" translates as "nothing but," "ta" as "to hit" and "za" as "to sit," or "nothing but to sit to hit".

The metaphor is of a swordsman engaged in a fight with a skilled opponent, something for which Zen training was widely used in ancient Japan. There can be nothing in his mind for if he was distracted even for a second he would be killed. He must be ready to strike or deflect an attack at any time. Thinking about his next meal, a geisha which awaits the victor, or the prize or honor he might receive, will likely be his demise.

This is the level of attention required for this sitting meditation, just sitting with an empty mind but with complete and heightened awareness.

The practices described in this book can bring you to a state in which you have an empty mind but with complete and heightened awareness, but without effort. You can discover that far from requiring such extraordinary effort as the sword fighter or Zen meditator in shikan taza, it is your natural state, in fact what you already are.

How many thoughts do you have and how long can you go without thinking?

Sit comfortably, and without straining or effort, just be still and count, for five minutes, how many thoughts arise.

This is a useful indicator as to where you are in your work. As this counting is done, it can create the feeding ground for the mind's endless comparisons, judgments, guilt, pride, etc., also just more thoughts. What suppression and replacement techniques do you try to stop the thoughts? How many intervals are there when you have no thoughts and are simply at peace, still and aware?

How many thoughts did you count in five minutes? Ten, a hundred, or did you just give up? The average person has something like 60,000 thoughts per day, or about one for every second they are awake. Are this many thoughts really necessary? Do you really think up, consider the outcomes of, and decide what to do with your 60,000 thoughts per day?

Imagine how many thoughts the 6,600,000,000 people on the earth have every day. If my math is correct, that is something like 396,000,000,000,000,000 thoughts per day per earth. Are all of these thoughts really necessary? Are they making things better, more stable, more peaceful? Is it really believable that each of those thoughts is carefully conceived, considered, weighed and decided upon every day?

Practically, how would it work if each of the world's 6,600,000,000 people had free will, could predict all outcomes of their actions on all other people, and could get what they wanted? Is this what really happens? What would it look like on a global scale?

As you are able to become more present, you will find that thoughts slow down. You may find that the very act of counting and noticing the thoughts slows them down, perhaps dramatically. Simple awareness seems to function like a sort of Heisenberg uncertainty principle from quantum physics. In quantum physics, a fundamental principle is that you cannot know both characteristics of a particle, position and momentum, simultaneously. If one is known perfectly, the other cannot be known. Somewhat similarly, if there is complete, total awareness of consciousness (position), then there is no energy (momentum) for thoughts to emerge, and surprisingly long periods can pass without thought.

Realizing that your natural state is stillness, that you are not your thoughts, and not an I, changes the game entirely, however. If I am not very tired, my thoughts will be at the level of a handful or so in an hour, hour after hour, despite what I am doing. In fact, the best indicator of how tired I am is whether or not thoughts are present. As someone who could have been a charter member of Thinkers Anonymous, this is a dramatic change. For a long time, my thoughts were like one of those horror movies where thoughts are birds and I am trapped in a phone booth being attacked by flocks of them. Now, it is an empty sky with the occasional few birds flying across high up and not landing.

Everything happens just as it happens, and what needs to occur, occurs, what needs to be said, is said. This is true whether it is a presentation at a business meeting, a meditation class or a cup of tea. As thoughts arise, they arise from and pass away in stillness, with no one there to grab hold of them.

Just how important is it to be able to concentrate on one thought or to have fewer thoughts? Ramana, in response to the question, "… are there any signs…which will indicate the aspirant's progress towards Self-realization?" replied, "The degree of freedom from unwanted thoughts and the degree of concentration on a single thought are the measure to gauge one's progress."

Can you predict and control your thoughts?

Next, let's focus on your ability to control and predict your thoughts. Make certain that you are in a still and centered space. If you need to, take several deep breaths focusing on the exhales, perhaps counting them to bring you into the present with awareness.

This simple exercise is to predict what you will think for the next five minutes. Write down on a piece of paper your predicted thoughts in as much detail as you can. As you are in control of your thoughts, this should not present any difficulty. Now, put down the paper, and sit still, calm and focused and see what your thoughts actually are for the next five minutes.

Were your thoughts what you predicted only five minutes earlier? Were you even close to predicting what you would think about, let alone what exact thoughts you would have? Did you try any techniques to make it come out like you predicted, like remembering some special place, experience or mantra that you thought you could hold on to? Did it work? How long did it work?

What does this tell you about your thoughts and how much you are in control of your thinking? If you aren't able to predict your thoughts or control them, what does that say about your ability to make decisions or to come to logical conclusions?

A related exercise is to try to not think about something. Take something unusual, even preposterous, which you would normally not encounter and would never even think about like a giraffe or a hippopotamus. Once you have chosen your object that you will not think about, see if you can not think about it for five minutes.

How long were you able to go without thinking of the giraffe? Did you find any techniques to suppress the giraffe thought? Did they work and if so, for how long? Did fighting against the giraffe thought stop it, or make it come up? Once the giraffe thought came up, did it go away, or did it keep coming back despite your best efforts?

Again, what does this tell you about your ability to control your thoughts? If you can't predict your thoughts and aren't even able to not think about something, why do you feel you are in control of your thoughts?

Where do your thoughts come from? Where do they go?

Continuing with the investigation, starting from a still, meditative space, with your breath long and calm, pay close attention not to the thoughts themselves, but only to where they come from. Try to catch a single thought as it is formed and watch it carefully as it rises up into consciousness. If the thought stream is too fast, and the start of a particular thought is missed, keep returning to your breath, making it long, slow and deep, and continue watching until you are able to watch one thought arise. Continue for five minutes.

Then shift your attention to where the thoughts go as they fade away. This is normally easier as you have something to start with, something to hold on to and watch disappear. As before, if the thoughts are moving too fast, return to your breath and lengthen and still it, focusing on the exhales. Go back to focusing on the thoughts and see if you can isolate one and watch it disappear. Continue for five minutes.

Where do your thoughts come from? Where do they go? Do you think them up, or are they created from nowhere, out of your control? Do you decide when they should end, or do they end by themselves whenever they happen to end, controlled by no one?

In your day-to-day life, watch when you are trying to decide between several alternatives. Where did the thoughts that are these particular choices come from? A week ago, did you think that this decision would be here exactly as it is? Can you bring forth the thoughts of all of the outcomes of your choices on any alternative path?

If you can't control what your thoughts will be, don't know where they come from or go to or when they will end, why do you feel that you can control your life? Who is really in charge?

What is this "I"? Does it change or is it constant?

An interesting exercise is considering what your "I" is and whether or not it changes with time, situation, environment, age, etc. Visualize your "I" as an entity, and then imagine what it might look like under those conditions. As an example, below are four different conditions that an "I" might undergo and how it might feel in each situation. If your "I" does change like this, is it a constant well-defined entity or a constantly changing cascade of situational, ad-hoc characters?

I REALLY AM SOMEBODY

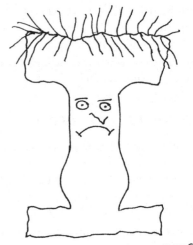

IT JUST ISN'T WORKING

ASSISTANT SECOND V. P. SALES

AN OLD I

The "I" has many faces

If you find this exercise interesting and useful, I would strongly recommend that you get a copy of William Steig's *Strutters & Fretters*. He is a much better cartoonist than I will ever be and has a great grasp of the illusion of the self. The book is full of the many delightful guises of the self and exposes it for the ad-hoc comedy that it is.

These simple exercises can have a profound effect on your understanding of the mind and its operations. You have seen that a) thoughts are about the past and future, b) thoughts are unpredictable and beyond your control, c) most thoughts contain the I, d) trying to not think is difficult, e) thoughts are continuous, f) you can't predict your thoughts, g) you have thousands of random thoughts, h) your thoughts come from and go to emptiness, and i) your "I" is a changing cast of ad-hoc characters. These insights are critical to having the mind see its nature and, amazingly, and fortunately, begin to unravel itself from its craziness.

You will find that the mind is not an independent entity but just a jumble of random thought streams, and that thought is a tool and a sense much like hearing or seeing. If you internalize this understanding, your thoughts will rise with decreasing frequency and intensity as there are no hooks on them and no one to grab at them.

Thankfully, the mind, which is the source of all of these attachments, delusions and emotions can recognize its own unreality and disorder and begin to order itself in a simpler, clearer way. Recent brain-imaging work using functional MRI and positron-emission spectroscopy (PET) coupled with mindfulness-based cognitive-behavior therapy have shown remarkable effects on obsessive-compulsive disorder and depression. These approaches relied upon recognizing that we are not our thoughts and that often our thoughts and behaviors are the result of faulty brain circuitry or chemistry or mistaken beliefs. Given this understanding, the mind demonstrates a remarkable ability to constructively and holistically change its functional patterns. It is much easier to have the robber mind reform himself by recognizing that he is the problem, than it is to try to turn part of the mind into a policeman and use him to catch and punish another part of the same mind. In the latter process, there is a high degree of recidivism.

B. The Case for Practice in Awakening

There are some reputedly enlightened folk who have taught that there is nothing to be done as we are already enlightened. They further contend that all practice is meaningless and a diversion. Others say that practice is only useful to convince ourselves that we cannot get enlightened through practice. They believe that practice is done only so that we become so frustrated that we simply surrender our ego and its attempts, after which enlightenment just happens.

These viewpoints are reinforced by the lack of any apparent pattern or consistency to the situations in which enlightenment experiences occur. Some have been enlightened walking across a park, others when they kicked a stone against a bamboo and others when they visited a house of prostitution. Still others were awakened when they stepped off a curb or when they were waiting for a bus. In the author's case it occurred while doing a yoga posture that had been done thousands of times before. These unpredictable events which are clearly beyond any plausible cause and effect relationship are taken as proof of the impossibility of making enlightenment happen.

Similarly, the pattern and type of practice that preceded awakening is in some ways always different. Insisting that you follow precisely the path that worked for your teacher is guaranteed to be inadequate in some way. Any student, no matter how diligent and well-prepared is going to be different from the teacher in conditioning, experience, age, genetics, family history, bodily and mental capability, etc. How could something as complex and comprehensive as awakening not be a personally-tailored process?

There is an emerging scientifically-validated view on the necessity of practice that is gaining significant credibility. The traditional belief of neuroscience was that the brain was born with all of the neurons it was ever going to have and that experience or training did not change their functional pattern. However, neurophysiologic research on brain functioning is currently being done in legitimate scientific laboratories by top-ranked scientists with the latest tools. These tools include functional magnetic resonance imagining (MRI) and high resolution electroencephalography (EEG). These experiments demonstrate the existence of what has been called "neuroplasticity", or the ability of the brain to change its functional operational pattern with practice or experience. In this work, experienced meditators have a very different mode of processing sensory inputs and generating and controlling mental states than untrained, inexperienced people. It has been demonstrated that these untrained, inexperienced people can be trained in a relatively short time to show a change in their functional neural pattern as well.

In these studies, musical training has been used as a model for what happens with neuroplasticity. MRI studies on violinists have shown that the brain regions that control fingering movements grow in size; longer and more intensive practice produces bigger changes. How much training is required to generate meaningful changes in the brain leading to extraordinary capabilities in playing the violin? What about chess, Olympic sports, sculpting, etc. While there will always be the savants or the Mozarts, for the vast majority of us it is necessary to do lengthy and intensive practice. It was found that those at the top of their fields in many disciplines had significantly different associated muscle fibers, brain functional patterns and cognitive abilities.

For the violinists, those at the top level had practiced for about ten thousand hours; those at the next lower level about 7500 hours. The most extraordinary meditator in the most detailed neurophysiologic study had meditated for over 10,000 hours.

Surprisingly, decades before there were any sophisticated tools to demonstrate such a controversial and unexpected possibility, J. Krishnamurti often claimed that there was an "organic" change in the structure of the brain that accompanied enlightenment.

As a personal anecdote, my journey started with a totally unexpected and unprecedented (for me) dramatic spiritual experience with no preparation or practice. However, because there had been no preparation or practice, I just couldn't hold it; I was clueless. Despite much subsequent practice of yoga and meditation and other experiences, the page didn't turn until someplace in the 9,000 hours category for each, an approximation as I wasn't using a stop watch. Perhaps I am a slow learner of spiritual stuff, which is a distinct possibility. Perhaps my intellectual nature, training and professional life slowed things. Perhaps my practices were not additive, i.e. 1 + 1 = 1 ½. Perhaps my attachments were so heavily rooted that it took that long to let go. This is all mental speculation of no consequence. It was just as it was. It will be different for you. It does seem that my students are having an easier time than I had which is all to the good, although that too is just as it is.

If this research is correct it might explain why very few can perform any number of tasks at a transcendent master level without extensive practice. Without extensive reshaping of the neural patterns and functioning in the brain, the mechanics are not sufficiently patterned that transcendent creativity and performance can emerge, as Mihaly Csikszentmihalyi described in *Flow*.

This transcendent creativity has been described by many masters ranging from Cezanne and Picasso to Einstein, Crick (the discoverer of DNA), and Kekule (the discoverer of a key structure of much of biology). All of these masters were extremely proficient and well trained in their craft before they could be conduits for the transcendent insight and creativity. Picasso's and Michelangelo's early work demonstrated their consummate skill at crafting that would pave the way for their later expressions of transcendent creativity.

Indeed, there are few skills that do not require functional mastery before reaching the level at which the activity can become so automatic that something extraordinary or transcendent can occur. In something as prosaic as riding a bicycle, we start with a tricycle, graduate to a two wheeler with training wheels before removing the training wheels, riding with one hand and then no hands. Why would enlightenment be a chance occurrence made no more likely through some preparation?

Virtually all self-realized folk who proclaim that there is nothing that can be done in preparation for enlightenment, and who give adequate biographies, went through years of spiritual disciplines before the apparently serendipitous triggering event occurred. Isn't it more likely that there is a process that does modify the brain in a way that increases concentration and detachment and creates a different functional pattern?

Further support for the necessity of practice is offered by students who, with little practice or training have apparent enlightenment experiences. Unfortunately, their experience soon fades as there was no preparation of the neurological structure nor understanding or context within which to support the experience. The field had not been tilled so the sprout ultimately overwhelmed by weeds.

Ramana Maharshi, probably the most widely recognized enlightened sage of the 20th century awakened at the age of 16 with little prior spiritual training or inclination beyond casual exposure to some Hindu texts and temples and education in a Methodist school. Ramana achieved his awakening through inquiring into what his own death would be like.

Interestingly, even among those who have enlightenment experiences with little apparent prior preparation there is further support for the necessity of practice. The common observation by these enlightened folk who are open about their own process is that there is a settling in period of several years after enlightenment before realization is stable and clear. Perhaps this settling in period continues until a functional neural network repatterning process is completed.

Although Ramana had little preparation prior to his awakening, he spent many years after the experience meditating and remaining silent apparently grounding and stabilized the realization.

Ramana Maharshi described this as "Jnana, once revealed, takes time to steady itself.....the Self remains veiled by vasanas (latent impressions or tendencies) and reveals itself only in their absence.....To remain stabilized in it, further efforts are necessary." (1)

Ramana told countless seekers that each should pursue practices appropriate to their capabilities and interests. Although his focus with many was on meditative inquiry through questions such as "Who Am I?" and "From where does this I arise?" and recognizing that you are not this body, he encouraged others to work with mantras, reciting texts or devotional practices.

Among Ramana's close followers, the one best known in the West was H.W.L. Poonja, or Poonjaji. His clear teaching and understanding of Ramana's work were a critical element in my journey. Few teachers have been so straightforward and direct in communicating their understanding.

Poonjaji said in the latter part of his life "You do not have to practice any sadhana (spiritual preparation) ..." However, few spiritual aspirants could match Poonjaji's own intense sadhana.

At one point, Poonjaji would chant daily from 2:30 a.m. to 9:30 a.m. before going to work. After work, he would chant until he went to sleep. His standard practice was to do 50,000 recitations each day, synchronizing the chanting with his breathing. Poonjaji did many forms of traditional worship including reciting the names of the divine (japa) as well as mantras and prayers "with great fervor!" (2)

Poonjaji said that the turning point in his practice was when he realized from Ramana that he should have been asking the question "Who Am I?" all along.

Even a realized master who reaches the point that practice is no longer necessary went through exhaustive preparation and practice. Without his preparation, would Poonjaji have really understood the need for exploring the "I"? Were all of those hours of practice of no value in developing the concentration and detachment that allowed his transcendent understanding to emerge?

Stephen Harrison, another contemporary non-dualist teacher and writer, had a very similar experience. In his excellent book *Doing Nothing: Coming to the End of the Spiritual Search*, Stephen detailed how he "sought out every mystic, seer and magician" he could find anywhere. He described his twenty-five years of study of philosophies, severe austerities, periods of isolation and meditation. He concluded "... it was all useless."

Harrison described the recognition, similar to that of Poonjaji and of Ramana Maharshi, that the problem was that "Every experience, no matter how profound, was collected by the 'me'. The problem was the collector". (3)

Was that extensive preparation really useless just because it was no longer necessary? Isn't it possible that the practices gave him the ability to concentrate and detach so that he could recognize that the problem was the "me" and to then hold that understanding?

Similarly, Tony Parsons, a contemporary advaita teacher and the author of the outstanding *As It Is*, describes how hard he applied himself to "various disciplines, rituals and purifications". Tony states that his awakening happened "almost as if by accident" in walking across a park. (4) Isn't it possible that his spiritual work laid the framework for the triggering event to occur?

Spiritual teachers rejecting earlier practices as unnecessary seems no more reasonable than an Olympic high diver saying that since she no longer jumps off the side of the pool as she did as a beginner, that it was unnecessary. Similarly, a concert violinist would not claim that years of practicing scales and fingering were unnecessary as she no longer needs them.

Having the ability to recognize clearly that the problem is not the search but the one driving the search appears to require some training of the mind. Practice is necessary not just to recognize its futility, but also to develop the ability to concentrate and detach. With this learning, you can be the witness standing outside the mind, body and senses and see the real problem.

In response to questions about the necessity of effort in a practice to gain enlightenment, Ramana said "No one succeeds without effort. Mind control is not one's birthright. The successful few owe their success to their perseverance." (5)

C. How do you use physical postures (asanas) for awakening?

It may seem unusual to begin a series of practices for awakening/enlightenment with a section on physical practices. The body, however, lives in the mystery of your reality in a more immediate and intimate way than does the mind. In some ways, the mind is the more obscured and the body the clearer manifestation. As such the body represents for many folk a less encumbered door to realization. My own turning of the page occurred while doing an asana sequence using a meditative inquiry and affirmation.

Physical postures (asanas) are what most in the West think of when they hear the word "yoga". The *Yoga Sutras of Patanjali*, the historical codification of the principles of yoga, has 195 verses (sutras) but only 5 of them even mention the word "asana". As Patanjali stated in Chapter 1, Verse 2, "yogas chitta vritti nirodaha". This is often translated as "yoga is the stilling of the modifications of the mind". Swami Venkatesananda translates this sutra as "Yoga happens when there is stilling of the movement of thought—without expression or suppression—in the indivisible intelligence in which there is no movement."(6) Yoga is not about flatter abs, tighter buns, a perfect Pincha Mayurasana or being really comfortable in full lotus for an hour. Yoga is about stilling the cacophony of thoughts and achieving unending, natural, uncaused happiness and peace.

How many yoga classes really lead you to this state? How many yoga students realize that yoga can really end the psychological turmoil and chaos in their lives?

It is possible to weave non-dualistic self inquiry, negations, breath awareness and affirmations into an asana practice in a process of discovery that makes enlightenment a more likely happening. Unfortunately, most yoga classes are done with little recognition of this possibility. Little or no instruction is offered on the "inner game", the "Zen" of yoga, and the "stilling of the modifications of the mind".

In the posture flows (vinyasas) that are used in this work, the critical components are a) the sequencing of individual postures, b) the coordination of breath with movement, c) the smooth flow from one posture to the next and d) coupling inquiry, negation or affirmation with the breath and movement. The sequences are done in an attitude that is closer to prayer than to an athletic workout, even if they are done rapidly.

In many yoga classes, the meditative awareness which can be created is destroyed by doing postures in a broken fashion with little regard for a holistic sequence. There is much verbal instruction, stopping for alignment corrections and adjustments, getting and adjusting props, watching demonstrations, etc. There is also often the competitive environment created with levels, variations for some but not for others, having the most flexible student demonstrate asanas, etc. In a culture saturated with competition, this quickly creates in the student's mind yet another venue for comparison, judgment and angst, precisely the opposite of "stilling the modifications of the mind".

What kinds of postures should you use and how should you do them?

The three posture flows (vinyasas) shown in this section have been constructed to alternately expand and contract the breathing apparatus in a natural movement from inhalation to exhalation with alternating postures. The movement of lifting the arms, or stretching the front of the body, naturally leads to inhalation. Lowering the arms, or forward bending, naturally leads to exhalation.

Sequences should first be done 3 to 5 times without pauses. This will make the breath more regular and often lead to a calming of the mind. Whenever possible, the eyes should be closed. With the eyes open, we are more easily assailed by thought streams stimulated by interesting visual objects. Most minds, particularly in the West, are heavily visually oriented and not attuned to the sensations, sounds and energies in the body, let alone to simple awareness.

It is useful to initiate inhalation on opening postures from the front and top of the chest and to initiate exhalation on closing postures from the belly or abdomen. This facilitates a "top down" inhale moving from upper chest to the intercostals in the middle chest and then to the diaphragm/belly. Similarly the exhale is "bottom up" moving from diaphragm/belly to intercostals and then upper chest. This breathing sequence naturally supports what is happening in these flows. This initial focus engages and focuses the process of the breath for that half cycle as well as brings attention away from distractions and into the flow of the sequence. The breathing process is shown below:

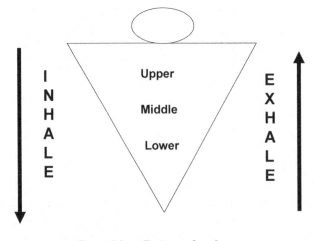

Breathing Pattern for Asana

It is important that you do the sequences throughout in a way that is well within your breath and physical capacity. If you are straining to achieve a flow which is beyond your abilities, your breath will be broken and rough and your movements choppy. This will shift the practice from a meditative stillness into comparison and striving and the resultant streams of thought.

If your physical and breathing capacities require you to make some accommodations in postures to do the sequence in a meditative, prayer-like state, then do them. This may involve bending your knees in forward bends, resting your knees on the ground in upward dog, shortening your stance, etc. You will find that many factors impact what is possible for you to do while maintaining the integrity of the sequence. When you are in your mind, straining, and have lost the ease and flow of your breath—that isn't it. When you are in a meditative stillness without physical straining and are within the ease and flow of your breath—that's it.

Develop some proficiency in the individual postures and in the entire flows before moving on to the more meditative aspects. When you are comfortable with the individual postures and the sequence then add some practices to increase your concentration during flows. Start with the classical Zen practice of counting your breaths. While this is often given as an introductory practice, it is elegant and powerful far beyond its simple appearance. Simply count your exhales.

If you are doing a flow without holds, count every exhale in the flow. If you are holding a particular posture, then count every exhale until you finish your holding or reach ten. If you reach ten, then restart at one. If you lose track or forget to count, go back to one. You can also count every inhale instead or both inhales and exhales, but counting exhales is normally more effective.

After you have developed some ability to concentrate through the breath counting, you can move on to inquiries. Inquiry is nothing more than asking a simple question which is interesting to you and which probes some of your commonly held assumptions and beliefs.

The question you select is important. Consider as possible choices, "Who am I?", "Where am I?", "When am I?", "What is doing this asana?", "What hears?", "What feels these sensations?", etc. You can come up with others of this kind, but the most important consideration is to determine which one is YOUR question. Some questions may feel too "philosophical", "equivocal", or "psychological". Others are too "obvious" or "uninteresting". Your question will have a "feel", an energy that gives you a sense of rightness, of "yes" arising out of your own deep intuition that this is THE question for you.

I found that "Where am I?" was particularly useful in my practice. As postures are done in space by an apparent body-mind and an apparent doer, it really worked with this practice. As sensations are constantly originating from different places in the body-mind, seeing if the I moves or where it is now as sensations change, can be a powerful vehicle for awakening. This does not imply that you should use the same question, but it worked for me and it has been effective for others as well.

Once you select a question, it is important to stay with it for a while. You may become bored with it, wonder if another question would be better, or consider abandoning the practice altogether. Persistence is the key. The mind will develop many reasons as to why this direct inquiry doesn't make sense. It doesn't want to be investigated or probed in this way; it is after all being threatened. Only by continued practice will the mind and the I loosen the hold that they have. The status quo has been the way it is now for a long time with a lot of external reinforcement; it isn't going to change overnight.

During the inhalations in the flowing postures, silently ask your question.

Allow it to sink deeply into your consciousness. This is not about getting the right intellectual answer, or saying it over and over again as a mantra. It is about feeling the question deeply within. With time, the inquiry will become a feeling, an intention, a deep questioning that is more a presence or energy than a thought. Moving into this phase takes the inquiry out of something that the mind is trying to understand and into the very structure and energy that is the "I" or ego.

After completing several sequences in this moving flow, try holding each posture in the flow for 3 to 5 breaths, or more, as you are comfortable, before moving on to the next one. If one particular posture feels particularly deep and still spend more time there. In Posture Flows (Vinyasas) I and III, postures A, B, C, D, and E can be held. In Posture Flow II, all postures can be held.

During this holding period, a second meditative approach can be used; negation, or "not this, not this" (neti, neti). This practice has been done for many millennia and is a cornerstone of awakening. As Ramesh Balsekar, a contemporary teacher says, "See the false as the false, and what remains is true ... Negation is the only answer to finding the ultimate truth—it is as simple as that."

With your eyes closed and your breath smooth and steady, during exhalations notice sensations or thoughts as they arise. As they arise, mentally repeat "Not this", or "I am not this". If you notice tightness somewhere, note the sensation, open to it, accept and welcome it with "not this". If a sensation or a thought stream arises, again "I am not this".

A starting point of this work is the realization that if you can recognize something else, or objectify it, you can't be that. You can't be the object you observe. You can't be in two places at the same time. You cannot both see your hands and be your hands. You cannot feel the tension in your shoulder and be that tension. The focus is on whether your identification with the body is correct or whether you are just the witness to the body-mind's functioning. This inquiry is a first step to moving towards what many call witness consciousness.

Don't resist or push the sensation or thought away as if you were afraid of it, as that resistance will only strengthen and validate it. Welcoming and acceptance softens the edges around the thought or sensation and opens the way for it to dissolve, to be absorbed in your simple awareness.

As with the inquiry during inhalations, the negations during holding will move from being mentally generated to becoming a feeling, an intention, or an energy operating in a deeper space. You will find that negations carry within them the question as to whether or not this is really true. Feeling within the negation the subtle but unmistakable presence of the implicit question opens the way to using that question as an inquiry.

You may want to try the inquiries and negations in Sanskrit. In your native language, you may be drawn into existing associations and linkages that create thought streams that lead you away from the inquiry. With spiritual roots and carefully-constructed phonics, Sanskrit has been demonstrated over millennia to have strong effects on the state of consciousness. Some linguistic scholars maintain that Sanskrit is a major source from which many of the Indo-European languages were derived. As such, it is buried deep within many languages but beyond the current neural associations and linkages.

Try substituting "Koham? (kho hum)" for "Who am I?", or "Kutam?" (khu tum) for "Where am I?" for inquiries. For negations, try "Naham ayam" (nah hum ah yum) or "Na aham" (nah ah hum) for "I am not this". Your intellectual left brain inquiry may be integrated and deepened with the sensing of the right brain triggered by the phonically-active Sanskrit.

Also, a deeper release or settling into a posture that you are holding often occurs with the "not this", than you get with a traditional "relax" message to tight areas. This is not surprising when you realize that much body tightness is the result of an I holding some emotion, pain or experience in the body as an object that it must deal with.

It can also be a powerful practice to simply focus on the breath during the posture flows. Watch the inhales and exhales closely. See if you can find where the inhale starts and where it goes to when it ends. Similarly with the exhale, where does it come from and where does it go to? Is there a space between breath cycles? Watch that space. Where are you when this space is there? If you are there, is the space there?

The creation of the I and its perceived job of protecting the body, which it regards as itself, from real and imagined physical and psychological dangers is the basis for most thought. This was an evolutionarily useful system to avoid saber-toothed tigers outside the cave, but in today's complex world, it is a strategy that is no longer useful or successful. Surrendering your manufactured fears and the I that holds them is critical to creating a more effective and holistic approach. Recognizing that the mind is unable to deal with the complexity of today's world is crucial. Thought creates more difficulties, dangerous behaviors, and stress than it avoids. Inquiry into the relationship between the mind, fear and the creation of the I is a key to enlightenment.

This approach can lead to the fundamental understanding that "I am not this body", not as a mental concept but as your lived reality. Few understandings will so surprisingly and dramatically alter the operation of thought as this clear and deep recognition.

How do you learn the posture flows?

Rather than attempting to start with an entire vinyasa, work first with the subparts of the vinyasa. For example, taking the first three movements of the posture flow shown below, work with them until the sequence becomes automatic. As already discussed, modify the postures so that you can do the flow within your breath capacity in a meditative, peaceful way. Then insert your inquiry on inhales during the flow and your negation during holding. When that becomes comfortable, add the cat stretch. Later, add "down dog" and finally "up dog." Remember to keep your eyes closed during the sequence; there is nothing to be seen or done outside—the work is on the inside. It's all happening in your mind.

There is no ideal rate at which learning these sequences should occur. Learn them as you learn them, recognizing the readiness of your body, breath and mind for the process. Do whatever number of steps you are working with well within your breath capacity in a meditative, prayerful, attentive state. Three steps done in a meditative state are preferable to six in a broken, breathless, scattered state.

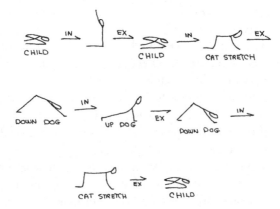

Each one of the vinyasas should be built up in the same fashion, chunk by chunk.

The Posture Flows
Posture Flow (Vinyasa) I.

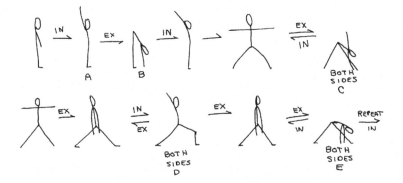

Posture Flow (Vinyasa) II

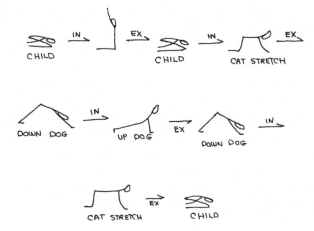

Posture Flow (Vinyasa) III

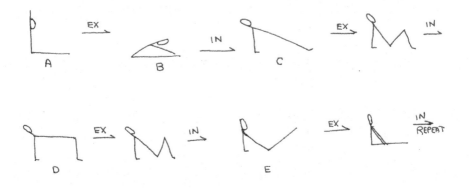

   These posture flows were selected as they tend to produce a meditative state conducive to meditative inquiry. It is possible to practice other well known flows such as the Sun Salutation in the same manner. Inquire as before on the inhales when you are moving. When you are holding an asana, use the negations on exhales. Synchronize breath to movement while maintaining the ease and awareness of a meditative state. Having done the Sun Salutation many, many thousands of times, it takes some proficiency before the flow can be done in an easy, peaceful, meditative way without thoughts.

   There are also many other different vinyasas that can also be used for meditative inquiry. These can be found in the books of Gary Kraftsow and Margaret and Martin Pierce in the Bibliography at the end. But don't get distracted by generating a host of flows. The three vinyasas shown here are sufficient for awakening.

   It may be helpful to visualize the method of doing these flows as similar to the way that movements are done in Tai Chi. In some Tai Chi classes, preparatory moves are done for some time until they done with ease and focus. Only then is the particular form undertaken. Performing a complete Tai Chi form without thought or effort and with complete awareness is challenging, just as one will find the practice described here.

What if you want to continue with your normal asana practice, how do you do that with inquiry?

If, after practicing the posture flows described, you are comfortable with the inquiry on inhales while moving and the negations on exhales during holding, you can extend the process to your normal asana practice.

Be alert as you move through your practice, inquiring on inhales and using the negations during holding. Be aware of sensations, thoughts or stress arising. As they arise, welcome each sensation in that silent awareness. Maintain awareness with the implicit inquiry, the "not this" energy, meeting what arises. Move through your practice in a meditative fashion, eyes closed, breath flow maintained.

If you have never tried it, this can also be an opportunity to see what naturally unfolds, what asana the body needs next. As your mind and doer move aside and are replaced by awareness, the body will express clearly what asana is really needed next. Go with it.

It will almost certainly not look like the same asana that you did yesterday, or it may be modified in a subtle or significant way. How long you hold it, if at all, will also be an exploration that arises from this opening. That is as it is NOW, not how it was in the past, nor how it will be the next time, nor what your mind thinks it should look like. Asana after asana, in whatever sequence or arrangement manifests, maintain the breath and inquiring awareness. When there is no next asana, the practice is complete; be still.

Working in this still awareness beyond mind and thought opens you to the body's inherent wisdom and stillness. As the body exists in the truth of being, this can be a powerful gateway to awakening.

How will you know if you're doing it right or making progress? What should you feel?

A useful marker as to how you are doing is if you can go through these simple vinyasas in continuous awareness without having thought streams distract you from the inquiry and negations. Have you moved from mentally repeating the inquiry and negations to their becoming subtle feelings? Can you be naturally and totally open and aware, just stillness, presence and emptiness throughout a flow? Can you go through a vinyasa without thought?

While these markers can give rise to dualistic comparisons and resultant thoughts, this work is about stilling the mind. If the mind isn't stilled, then work needs to continue.

As discussed earlier, asanas are often looked upon as only a physical exercise to be gotten through somehow, a workout to be done. Unfortunately, this robs practitioners of the great promise of yoga, that of union, stilling the mind, and completeness.

If you are doing asanas as part of a complete Patanjali ashtanga yoga approach focused on stilling the mind, the state of your mind in asanas matters. After all, breath control (pranayama), withdrawing your mind from the senses (pratyahara), concentration (dharana), and meditation (dhyana) are to bring about enlightenment (samadhi), a state beyond thought. The state of your mind while doing vinyasas is evidence as to what your pranayama, pratyahara, dharana and dhyana have really produced.

If your practice focuses on physical benefits and temporary stilling of the mind rather than a deeper realization, the mind will return in full when practice is over. Your asana practice, like your life, can become naturally peaceful and effortless, not through suppression or replacement, but through inquiry and understanding. If you cannot have a still, alert and clear awareness during asanas, there is no chance that you will have it in your daily life.

The posture flows indicated can be physically demanding, particularly if they are done rapidly or with many repetitions. It is important that anyone attempting them should be fully aware of their physical condition and capacity for exercise. Be aware of any medical limitations, including but not limited to blood pressure, skeletal and heart problems, etc. If there is any doubt, contact your health care provider. It is important that postures not be done to the point of pain; stretching will occur but if you feel pain, stop.

D. How should you sit for breathing, chanting and meditation?

You need to develop a comfortable posture for sitting, either on the floor or in a chair that allows you to remain alert and still for some time without pain or great discomfort.

If you are sitting on the floor, it is important to have the hips higher than the knees. The knees should be stable and supporting you by making contact with the ground, cushions, etc. The hips can be elevated with pillows or a meditation (seiza) bench so that the natural curves of the back are maintained without effort. Unless you maintain the natural concave curve of the lower back, the muscles of the back will be continuously working and eventually struggling to hold the body upright. This will eventually produce strain, unsteadiness, fatigue, discomfort and pain, no matter how strong your muscles are.

The legs should also be positioned to steady and support the body. It is important to do stretching postures to open the hips and groin and stretch the hamstrings. This will reduce the strain on the knees in whatever posture is selected for meditation. As we all know, knees do not bend to the sides. Many meditators and yoga practitioners and teachers have the scars to prove that they did not understand this. If the hips are not sufficiently opened and the hamstrings stretched, and you try to force or maintain your legs in some idealized posture, such as a full lotus, there is a high likelihood of injury.

Although the full lotus posture has some useful attributes, much of its value comes from having fleshy parts of the legs cushioning the body on a bare, hard floor. That is seldom the case in most meditation situations today. Often it is regarded as a rite of passage and done for ego-centered reasons with bad results. It is much less important to sit in the full lotus posture than it is to sit comfortably and with stability and awareness. I have been injured only a handful of times in 35 years of doing yoga and meditation; most of them involved the full lotus. You will be just as enlightened kneeling, sitting in simple folded leg postures or in a chair.

If you are doing a lot of sitting for many days, it is useful to have different complementary sitting postures in which you are comfortable. Alternating postures will minimize the stress on any particular joint or muscular area without compromising your intensity or awareness. Few Western practitioners are able to sit in full lotus for hours a day for many days without pain. Switch sides to balance the stress of sitting, i.e. don't always put the same leg on top in half lotus.

Recognize that structural imbalances in sitting postures can manifest in the neck, shoulders, upper back, and lower back, as well as the obvious hips, knees and lower back. A shoulder pain may really be a result of a tight groin muscle twisting the hips, for example.

Questions often arise as to the handling of pain during sitting and whether it isn't useful to teach detachment by confronting the mind with its typical avoidance mechanisms. Sitting with some discomfort for long periods of time without moving, as can be the case in the Zen tradition, does reveal the frantic nature of the mind to resolve what it perceives as a significant problem. However, if discomfort crosses over into pain, and most folk are aware of the difference, especially in the knees or lower back, injury can result that will require medical care. If the pain becomes acute, meditation ceases and pain management will be all that occurs in your sitting.

It is important to distinguish between pain and suffering. Pain is a message from the body that there is a physical problem that needs to be dealt with; suffering is the mind creating a story about the pain, about how terrible, irrational, or unfair this is. There can be suffering with little pain, and there can be great pain with no suffering. Recognizing the difference is a critical factor in meditation and in life.

A complete, balanced stretching program dealing with all parts of the sitting apparatus is important. This stretching is not just for more comfort in sitting for meditation. It is also critical to stretch and open the upper body, particularly the upper back, shoulders and chest for chanting and pranayama. Try chanting and pranayama with and without doing the Posture Flow II shown earlier before you begin and see the enormous difference. In addition to the posture flows in this book, many Zen and yoga books provide useful stretching exercises. A good teacher is also very helpful.

As to the question of how long to sit, the simple answer is "as long as you can", with the caution that it should not involve pain as described above. It is the experience of many practitioners that if you never sit for longer than 20 minutes, you are unlikely to see anything that looks like acceptable progress in sitting meditation. This is because it takes something like 10 or 15 minutes for most people to get their body and mind stilled and away from their previous activities. Consequently, you will likely eventually abandon sitting meditation as appearing to be of little value.

Many find that getting past 30 minutes is a critical tipping point in their practice and where changes really begin to occur. How long you are able to continue sitting productively can increase significantly with practice, but for most people something like 40 or 45 minutes is a good ending point, particularly if you are doing several rounds of sitting, alternated with 5 to 10 minutes of walking meditation or stretching.

In doing the walking meditation, called kinhin, there are some simple and powerful techniques. One that is particularly effective is to synchronize your steps with your breathing and then count your steps. See how many steps you take on each half breath cycle while maintaining a comfortable pace. You should not be breathless or straining even after walking for several minutes at this pace. If you get out of breath or feel uncomfortable, adjust it.

If you take two steps on each cycle, or two on inhales and three on exhales, then that is your pace. It will vary with terrain, your fitness, your concentration, etc. Some schools advocate certain ratios, but experiment with it. See what pace works for you and maintains a calm, peaceful, concentrated walking.

Count the steps in each half breath cycle. If you take two steps, then it goes on the inhale, "one, two". The exhale is similarly "one, two". There is no cumulative counting, just counting the steps in this inhale, then the steps in this exhale. You can also move to just watching the breath as your steps continue, but the breath counting is a useful technique for most folk regardless of their experience level.

E. How can you use the breath to awaken?

The breath has a powerful effect on the mind. As Ramana Maharshi describes in the 11th and 12th verses of *Upadesa Saram*:

11. *Control the breath and you control the mind.*

12. *Mind and breath, consciousness and action, are joined like two branches on a tree.*

Watching the breath and mind carefully, you can see that as the breath lengthens, slows and softens, the mind slows, and the thought streams become shorter and less intense. Whether you use sequences of postures coupled with inhalation and exhalation as described earlier, or practice breathing exercises (pranayama), a dramatic change in the mind occurs. With this understanding, many excellent windows into awakening have been found over the millennia.

An important first step is to focus on how inhales and exhales are done. There are three main regions of the breathing apparatus, a) the clavicles and upper chest, b) the main chest and intercostal muscles and c) the diaphragm or belly region. The amount of air moved and the deepness of the breath increases as you move from a) to c), i.e. diaphragmatic breathing is the deepest and moves the most air. All three regions are engaged in what is called a complete yogic breath. It is helpful if you try to do these separately so that you can recognize each one. Placing your hand on your belly, intercostal muscles or shoulders while you breathe is a useful way to isolate and observe each in operation.

There is much debate about exactly how inhales and exhales should be done and in which sequence for pranayama. Gary Kraftsow describes five different types of inhale, for example.

Many senior teachers (which means those that the author agrees with) recommend doing pranayama by inhaling "from the top down", i.e. upper chest to belly, and exhaling "from the bottom up", i.e. belly to upper chest. This would be the first approach recommended. This pattern is shown below:

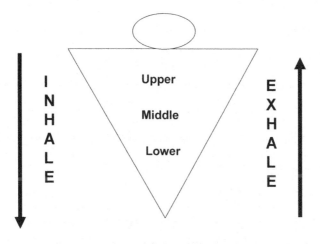

Breathing Pattern for Pranayama

Others recommend inhaling "from the bottom up", and exhaling "from the top down". As we will discover later, this approach has advantages in chanting. In chanting, leaving the contraction of the diaphragm to the end of the exhale naturally creates a gentle lock that lengthens and smoothes the chant. It is less advantageous in pranayama, however.

As to the length of the inhale and exhale, an important guideline is to focus more on the exhale than the inhale. If your exhale is rough and jagged and leaves you gasping for the next inhale, you need to back off until you reach a place where you can practice with comfort and ease. The exhale should be at least as long as the inhale. Preferably, and naturally for most, it will be longer.

There are some excellent discussions on the breathing apparatus and other breathing practices in the books mentioned in the Bibliography. As with physical postures, recognize that the breath is a powerful tool. If it is misused, or highly stressed, it is possible to injure yourself, physically or mentally. Remember the injunctions with regard to consulting one's physician and being alert to issues such as cardiovascular limitations as well as others.

Counting the breaths—just how difficult can that be?

A classical approach from Zen meditation is to count your breaths. To begin with, count both the inhales and the exhales. Breathing consciously and slowly, count each half of the breath cycle from 1 to 10 and then again return to 1. If you are pulled away by thoughts and lose your place, return to 1 and begin again.

How successful are you at reaching 10 without losing count? Is this more difficult than you expected? What does this tell you about your mind?

Notice the state of the mind and the breath when you begin the practice. Then, after doing the practice for a while, observe it again. How is it different? What does your mind feel like? Are you more still or less still? Are the thought streams as intense? Are there as many thought streams?

After some practice with counting both the inhales and exhales, shift your focus to the exhales and count just them. Notice the state of the mind when you begin, and then again after some time. How is it different from when you were counting both inhales and exhales? Are you more still or less still? Are there as many thought streams? How does the mind feel?

Now repeat the exercise while counting just inhales. Again, what happens with the mind and thought streams? How is it different from counting exhales?

Counting the breath is a fundamental and powerful meditation approach. At a well-known Zen center at which I practiced, the roshi gave this practice to all participants in a week long meditation intensive (sesshin). This was the practice for all, even though many practitioners had been meditating for years with other techniques. While at first it appears simple, even trivial, this practice will be surprisingly difficult for most practitioners. Being unable to count your breaths without forgetting what number you are on is a revealing practice. This discovery that your mind isn't as much under your control as you believed can be an important one.

This practice can also be of great value in daily life when the mind begins to race, or becomes trapped in a tight, emotional, obsessive loop of thoughts on a single topic. When this occurs, turn to the breath and the simple counting of exhales. See if the obsessive loop doesn't slow down, replaced by shorter and slower trains of thoughts on other topics. Whatever the situation or the emotion, the breath is a powerful tool to grab the reins of the wild rider-less horse of the mind.

How do I use breathing exercises with inquiry to go deeper?

As Ramana Maharshi says in the 14th verse of _Upadesa Saram_:

Lasting control of the mind can be accomplished by stilling it through breath control, then contemplating That.

The next step in using the breath as a meditation practice is to begin carefully watching it.

Sit in a comfortable, steady meditative posture in which you can remain still for some time. Slow and deepen the breath until it becomes regular and even with the exhale as long as or longer than the inhale.

Pay close attention to what happens at the end of an exhalation. Without any forceful retention or straining, be aware of the mind as the exhalation ends, before the inhalation begins. Watch the exhalation tail off and softly end.

Where does it go? What does it disappear into? Be watchful as the energy of the exhalation ends and before the inhalation begins. Is there a space there? What does it look and feel like? What is thought doing?

Shift your attention to the beginning of the inhalation. Watch carefully its source. Where does it come from? What causes it to come into being? What initiates it? What happens to the energy of the mind?

Next, as the inhalation continues, watch as it expands and then comes to an end, without your holding or straining, watch it tail off. Where does it go? Is there a space there before the exhalation begins? When the exhalation begins, where does it come from? Who initiates it?

What happens to thought at these turnings of the gate of the breath, this ending of one movement and the beginning of the next? Is it like the turning that occurs with an arrow shot up into the sky, going upward until eventually it stops and then turns and falls? Are you there when the arrow stops at the peak? What is in that space?

This powerful meditative approach using something that you do thousands of times every day is always available, free of charge. It has been used for thousands of years. It is an open window hung on a wall that isn't there. Answering these few questions in these simple exercises can be the only practice you will ever need on your path to awakening.

Are there questions that can be used for meditative inquiry with breathing exercises?

Ramana Maharshi outlined a practice for meditative inquiry with breathing exercises using a classical negation, an inquiry, and an affirmation:

Inquiry	*Koham*	Who am I?	inhalation
Affirmation	*Soham*	I am That	retention
Negation	*Na aham*	I am not this	exhalation
Affirmation	*Soham*	I am That	retention

As was done with the posture flows, use this inquiry, affirmation, negation and affirmation cycle as you do normal breath cycles. Make the breaths long and slow, close your eyes, and feel the inquiries, affirmations and negations. Watch the mind. What happens to your thoughts? Is there a question in the affirmations and negations? Does the mind try to come up with an answer? Does your mind sometimes freeze at being unable to do something with this practice? Watch that space and see how the mind hurries to fill it with something acceptable or anything at all, just to avoid that emptiness. What is the mind afraid of? What does it fear will happen if that space remains?

It is also possible, although more difficult, to do these exercises in more complex breathing exercises like kapalabhati, anuloma, viloma, and pratiloma ujjayi and nadi sodhana. Before you attempt to insert the inquiries, you should have developed comfort and ease in working with these more difficult pranayamas. The guidance of a capable teacher is recommended. These complex breathing exercises can distract you from the meditative inquiry and it is the inquiry, not the pranayama, which will set you free. You will not be more enlightened because you know the complex breathing exercises.

F. How can you use chanting to awaken?

Ramana Maharshi's meeting with a master of Sanskrit and non-dual philoso-phy (Vedanta) named Ganapati Muni, speaks to the effectiveness of chanting as an avenue for awakening.

At the time, Ramana had been living in silence for 11 years in a cave on a mountain (Arunachala) in south central India. One hot fall afternoon, Ganapati Muni was in despair over his inability to achieve Realization despite enormous efforts. He had spent many years visiting sacred places, performing ascetic prac-tices, memorizing texts, reading extensively, arguing Vedanta philosophy, and performing mantras and invocations. He rushed up the hillside to see the sage, who was now in his late twenties, and still called by his given name, Venkataraman. Ganapati Muni fell at his feet, clasped them in his hands and said that despite all his efforts, he still did not understand what spiritual practice (tapas) was. He begged Venkataraman to tell him the nature of true spiritual prac-tice.

Ramana looked at him silently for about fifteen minutes and then said only two sentences, the last of which was "When a mantra is repeated, if one watches the Source from which the mantra sound is produced the mind is absorbed in That; that is tapas (spiritual practice)". (7) Ganapati Muni was overwhelmed and awakened by this insight, and in recognition of this renamed the sage Bhagavan Sri Ramana Maharshi.

Using mantras not just as devices to focus and entrain the mind, but instead focusing on that place from which they emerge, and into which they dissolve, can open the door to awakening. In my experience, particularly powerful chants for this approach are Vedic chants, which are often over 3,500 years old and spring from the Vedas, the classical texts of Hinduism. They are relatively simple, have been phonically tuned in Sanskrit to have a great impact on the mind and have stood the test of time. Sanskrit is also powerful as it is one of the root languages for most Western languages, so there is a felt sense of it. However, since Sanskrit is not your native tongue, it induces fewer mental associations and diversions than would chanting in English. Some of these chants have been chanted by mil-lions of people over thousands of years.

Chanting is more effective if your breathing is focused as to how each inhale and exhale is done. Inhales are most effective for chanting if they are done from the "bottom up", i.e. first using the diaphragm, then the ribs, then the upper chest. Exhales during chanting are most effective if they are done "top down", i.e. first using the upper chest, then the ribs, and then the diaphragm. You will find that if you leave the contraction of the diaphragm to the end of the exhale, that this naturally creates support and a gentle lock on the energy in the lower part of your body. This approach smoothes and lengthens your chanting. To prove that this breathing approach is preferable, try doing it the opposite way, i.e. chant on the exhale from the "bottom up" and see if your chanting is as long and smooth. This breathing approach, which is different from what is normally recommended for pranayama, is used by many singers, chanters and students of Indian music for just this reason. This breathing pattern is:

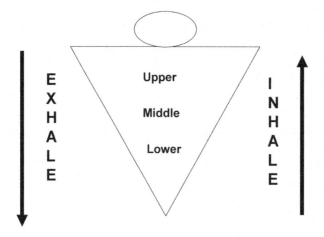

Breathing Pattern for Chanting

We will explore three classical Vedic chants and look at what they mean, and what tonal arrangements are most effective. Russill Paul, in his excellent *The Yoga of Sound: Tapping the Hidden Power of Chant and Music*, lays out the approach of using three tones for Vedic chanting and prescribes the arrangements used here. It can deepen your practice if the lowest tone is focused deep in the belly, in what is known as the lower chakras or hara, designated Ha. The intermediate tone is focused in the region of the heart or middle chakras, designated He. The upper tone is focused on the region of the forehead, brow, upper chakras or third eye, designated Te. Chanting in this way can activate the energies in those regions.

As the original Vedic texts have no prescribed tonal arrangements for these chants, arrangements can vary a great deal. Some of these chants are widely used, even in contemporary music, with their own unique tones and beats.

Rather than use separate phonic markings for the Sanskrit sounds which you would have to learn and translate, the sounds are given approximately as they sound when they are presented in their tonal arrangements. Listening to actual recordings will also help. What is given here is about 92.37% correct. It will capture the power of the Sanskrit without being more complex and problematic than most Western students want to deal with.

The meditative impact of all Vedic chants you will work with is strengthened if each line is chanted on one out breath, followed by a silent inhale. An alternative approach for deep work is to chant a line on the exhale and then whisper the next line on the inhale so that the chant goes on continuously. Another powerful routine is to move sequentially inward with more and more subtle chanting on subsequent rounds, first chanting out loud, and then whispering, and then finally chanting internally in silence.

These chants are classically done a minimum of three times, but can be done as many times as you are moved to do.

Asato Ma

Asato	ma	sat	gamaya,	Tamaso	ma	jyotir	gamaya,
Non-being	to	being	lead me	darkness	to	light	lead me

Mrtyur	ma	amritam	gamaya
Death	to	eternal bliss	lead me

This chant is an asking to be led from the non-being of ignorance to the being of realization, to be led from the darkness of ignorance to the light of understanding, and to be led from the death of ignorance to the eternal bliss of knowledge.

Classically, this request was being made to your teacher, God, guru, etc. However, in using these to awaken to the Oneness that we already are it is used in a different, non-dualistic (not two) context. The request is being made by the ego to the ground of all being, Oneness, Presence, etc. It is your personal I asking for help to awaken, your self beseeching your Self. This chant can be a powerful expression of surrender, of the recognition that you can't do it by yourself.

Te		mah			mah		
He	tho			gah		yah	
Ha	Ahsah		sadh				

Te			mah		gah	mah	
He		sew		teer			yah
Ha	Thah	mah		jyo			

Te			mah		gah	mah	
He		your		tham			yah
Ha	Mree<u>th</u>		ah mree				

This chant has been used as background music for the credits in a recent movie, Matrix III. The arrangement shown above, which is very different from the movie credits version, has been an effective one for many people.

Lokah Samastha

Lo kah	sa mas ta	sukhi nu	bha van tu
Worlds	all/whole	peace/happiness/well-being	wish/meditate/may

May all beings in all worlds (on all planes) have peace, happiness and well-being.

This chant, which is often known as the "Peace Chant", has been used for millennia in many places by many folk to capture that feeling. There are many arrangements. Russill Paul's approach is shown below.

Te						bha van	
He		kaah		tha		new	thu
Ha	Low		sah mahs	sueke			

This chant is most powerful when chanted completely on an exhale, followed by a silent inhale and is classically done three times at a minimum.

While this chant is traditionally used to ask God, Buddha, Jesus, the Ultimate Reality, etc., to give peace and well-being to all beings in all worlds, it can also be directed in different ways. It is often focused in a series to someone close to you, then to someone with whom you are having some difficulty, and then to yourself (often the most abused and mistreated of the three). It can be powerful to direct this chant to the person you dislike the most, whether it is a politician, world leader, criminal, or someone closer. Seeing if you can really wish well-being to someone you dislike intensely can be a powerful test of whether or not you really understand that everyone is One and a Buddha. Your sense of "yes, this too, even this" will be tested. The world, from an awakened perspective can be seen as a creation of your own mind. In doing this chant for you to find peace within your-self, you are in fact, at the deepest level, working on the peace of the entire world.

Krato Smara Krutam Smara

Krato	*smara*	*krutam*	*smara*
God/the Universe	please remember	all that I have done	please remember

The literal translation for "krato" is "the one for whom the deeds are done". There are four different tonal sequences in this arrangement which make for a powerful vehicle. Some of my students have described this arrangement as "sticky", as it does engage and hold you in an unusually strong way.

Te						
He	Krah	tho	smah rah	kru thahm	smah rah	
Ha						

Te		tho				
He			smah rah	kru thahm	smah rah	
Ha	Kra					

Te		tho	smah rah	kru thahm	smah rah	
He						
Ha	Kra					

Te						
He		tho	smah rah	kru thahm	smah rah	
Ha	Kra					

While this chant is often used classically to make certain that God remains aware of what you have done so that He/She will reward you appropriately, it can also be used in non-dualistic work. The doer of the deeds, as well as the one who insisted that they be done, exist only in your mind. Remembering that, surrender all that was done and who it was that wanted them done.

A powerful practice is to do three rounds of all four tonal sequences, again chanting a complete line on each exhalation with a silent inhale.

Working with this chant can be done with no specific intent, surrendering whatever arises in consciousness. It can also be powerful to focus on something or someone you are deeply attached to, past experiences of which you are proud or ashamed, or working your way through a text like Nirvana Shatakam. As each is brought into consciousness, it is surrendered. The surrender can be to a guru, to the Void, to a mentally envisioned fire, to the sun, etc. which absorbs and consumes it. What is being surrendered is not the experience, item, person, relationship, or emotion, but your attachment to it.

You may move into chanting with a still mind so that there is the sound of the chant and its resonance, but there is no mentation about the intent or meaning of the words of the chant. The work is then being done by the energy of the chant, and your intention and feeling of inquiry.

As the chants are done, watch the mind. What happens to the mind as the chanting continues? See if you can see, as Ramana suggested, where this chant comes from. Can you see where the chant goes to when the sound dies away? Who is doing this chant? If you chant for some time, you may have the experience that the chant is doing itself, that there is no one making the sound. What does that say about you? Where are you then?

There are countless chants that span every religious and spiritual tradition as well as the length of man's apparent existence. Although Sanskrit chants have unusual power, as discussed earlier, there are many powerful chants in other languages and traditions, including English. The most important thing is to find the chants that resonate with you and work with them.

Recordings of these chants are on the author's website at www.happiness-beyond-thought.org. Excellent recordings and the backgrounds of these chants on CDs and in print are available at www.russillpaul.com.

G. Meditative Inquiry—Where the rubber meets the road

Meditative inquiry, the direct questioning of long held beliefs through attempting to answer simple, fundamental existential questions, forms the basis for much of this work. Ramana Maharshi, in his early 20s, gave responses to questions which became the text, *"Who Am I?"*, one of the most succinct and direct discussions on how this work is to be carried out. In one portion, he gives this summary of meditative inquiry:

"When other thoughts arise, one should not pursue them, but should inquire: 'To whom do they arise?' It does not matter how many thoughts arise. As each thought arises, one should inquire with diligence, 'To whom has this thought arisen?' The answer that would emerge would be 'to me'. Thereupon if one inquires 'Who am I?' the mind will go back to its source and the thought that arose will become quiescent. With repeated practice in this manner, the mind will develop the skill to stay in its source." (8)

We will now explore just how you go about this process in your awakening.

Are there any physical practices that would help you with your inquiry?

In addition to the earlier general guidelines for breathing exercises, chanting and meditation, a different breathing pattern is normally recommended for meditation. It is useful, many schools would say very important, to breathe predominantly in the belly, or with the diaphragm. This is illustrated by:

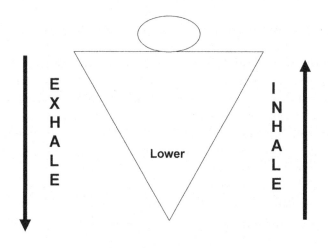

Breathing Pattern for Meditation

By breathing predominantly in the lower abdomen, also called the hara or lower chakras, you will find that the mind is likely to be more still and your attention more focused.

What question should you use for the inquiry?

In addition to "Who am I?" there are a number of questions that can be fruitful ground for investigation. These include "Where am I?", "When am I?", "What am I?", "Why am I?", "Who hears?" etc. Ramana stresses in Upadesa Saram the value of the inquiry "From where does this 'I' arise?" as a powerful practice, summarized in the English spoken during Ramana's time as "Whence am I?".

Don't worry about the specific purpose of each different question and its implications and whether you need to exhaust every possible question. In much experience in working with these, I have found that the differences are more apparent than real. The end point is the same in each case. Your interest in the particular question chosen should guide your decision. A question that is of little interest to you is of no value in your practice simply because you won't do it.

In determining THE most useful question, some questions may appear to you to be too philosophical, equivocal, or psychological. Others look to be too obvious or uninteresting. The ones that are most powerful and provide important keys to the doors are those for which you have a feel, an energy that gives a sense of rightness, of "yes" arising out of your own deep intuition that this is THE question, that it is YOUR question.

The classical practice of having a teacher, guru, roshi or seer of some sort assign mystically the question (koan in Zen practice) psychically selected for that particular seeker works to the extent that the seeker believes that it is the right question and that it must be followed. This belief reduces the customary doubts that will invariably arise as the practice progresses and the mind resists the inquiry.

An experienced and perceptive teacher who has done many years of different practices, dealt with many students, and knows this particular student well, will be likely to assign a useful question, although it may still not be the right one. It is most important that it comes from the teacher's emptiness and stillness. Some groups assign to a relatively unknown folk, after a brief ceremony, payment of fees, and an offering, a mantra from a very short list that, not surprisingly, is kept secret. You will find that many others have been assigned this same secret mantra. This approach is unlikely to be of much value to the practitioner.

In my own practice, I was originally assigned a koan to work with that was the standard initial practice of that particular roshi. It just really didn't engage me or work for me at any level, even after much time and effort. I met with the roshi and said that I had another question (one of the ones listed above) that felt deeply right for me, and he accepted it. It was a critical turning point in my practice.

Once you have selected your question, you should work with it with a lot of diligence and hold it in attention for a significant length of time. You should work on this question intensively for several months before you reject it and select another option. You will find that the mind, anxious to derail this process, will quickly become bored with a particular question and then will suggest another, and another, and yet another in quick succession. Resist this. Sinking into the question, to the root and feel of it, absorbing yourself so completely in it that it goes on by itself, even while you are asleep, requires single-minded dedication and focus on one question.

OK, you have your question, now what do you do?

Sitting in meditation with your question, you do not merely repeat the question mechanically over and over again like a mantra hoping to dull the mind. Using a question, such as "Where am I?" you ask the question deeply and attentively. Feel the question and allow it to sink down into the depths of your consciousness. As other thoughts or sensations emerge, ignore them, no matter how spiritual, illuminating, frightening, inspiring, repulsive or attractive they might be. Again, ask the question, "Where is the I that has this thought?"

As you feel some part of the body, a sensation, an external object, or a thought, see exactly where the I is that is seeing that and where it came from. Move your focus to the object of your seeing, and look back at that place where the apparent seer was just located. Where is the seer now located? Is there an I there, or anywhere? Or is it all a phantom, a conditioned mental response?

The "From where does this 'I' arise?" inquiry can also be approached by repeating your name, silently or out loud, and looking for where it arises. This was a favorite practice of the famous English poet, Wordsworth. Feel the energy around the sounding of your identifier, the sound that you respond to as who you are. What is the space in which it arises? Where does the name go when it passes from consciousness? What energy and associations are attached to that one particular sound? Is it a clear, simple sound or does it have imbedded within it feelings, pains and pleasures, regrets and joys?

What if you say the name of a friend, partner, parent, sibling, or boss? Can you see the bundling of mental constructs, the lightning rod that is attached to these labels, and all that it brings with it? What gives this sound such potency? Is it the sound itself, or the mind with its memory and associations?

Similarly with the I, me or mine. Say each of them silently or aloud. Feel its energy, and where it comes from. Where exactly in the body or mind does it originate? Is it always the same place? Does it always come with the same energy and associations, or does it vary from time to time? Is the I a constant entity or is it a glued-together assemblage of ad hoc creations?

Be watchful as to what occurs immediately after you ask your question. Often, immediately after the question is asked the mind will just stop and emptiness and stillness will be there. This is the Presence that you are searching for. Don't rush past it looking for another answer. There isn't an answer the mind can come up with. The mind will often panic at not having an answer and not understanding what just happened with the stillness will quickly rush to fill in the blank space with all sorts of other possibilities.

This is why questions with less obvious alternative answers like "Where am I?" are more useful than more philosophical ones like "Who am I?" where the mind can quickly construct myriad possible answers for consideration after its initial failure. Watching this process is a key insight into how mind operates.

When should you do the inquiry?

A critical, and unique aspect of this approach is that meditative inquiry is not confined to the time you have available to spend sitting still in a meditative posture. The process can continue sixteen (or twenty four) hours a day, seven days a week in whatever you are doing. As you extend the meditation from the defined period of a sitting practice into your daily life, select a daily periodic activity to trigger you to reengage with the question. This reminder, whether it is answering the phone, beginning eating, going to the bathroom, traveling to work, having a cup of tea, every odd numbered hour, etc. will move you back into the depths and immediacy of your inquiry.

It is particularly powerful if you use the inquiry as the first thing on waking to establish the tone for the day and the last thing before falling asleep to place it into consciousness so that it will continue during the night.

With inquiry of this intensity, before long, things will begin to change in your life, some subtle, some not so subtle. There is the misconception that nothing happens until the BIG BANG of enlightenment. Nothing could be further from the truth. Your heart will be lightened before, and whether or not, an enlightenment event ever happens. Focusing your process on getting a special experience that you can tell your friends about as soon as possible can significantly hinder your work. Creating a powerful ego to drive to a goal is the very ego that you will in the end need to discard to reach beyond the mind.

You do not suddenly master playing the piano, speaking a foreign language, rock climbing, painting abstract art or doing mathematical equations. You get better and more effortlessly capable as you continue your practice and as your concentration, capacity and understanding develop, whether or not you become Picasso, Einstein or flawlessly fluent in French—so it is with meditative inquiry.

What if you get bored? When should you change your practice?

Your practice will at times be unpleasant and feel hard and dry. You will feel like it is not moving as you think it should be in a continuously upward trajectory. You will see parts of your mind and thoughts that surprise, disappoint, frighten and depress you in greater profusion than you were ever aware of before. Inquiry has not somehow mysteriously created them. They were there all along. With everything else out of the way, they now have a chance to manifest. With persistent inquiry, your thoughts will lose their strength and energy. Some may still come back repeatedly. Eventually they will have smaller, duller hooks than they used to have to snag you and pull you into an obsessive stream of thoughts. They will trouble you less and less.

You may also find, even after you have apparently achieved some progress and perhaps had some spiritual experiences that practice will appear to have stalled, become lifeless, and lost its capacity to engage you. When this occurs, persist for some time. See if it is just the mind's resistance and conditioning trying to derail the process. Leave the inquiry alone for a while and take a break and then return to it. See if your interest in the inquiry has returned.

If not, see if it is time for the next step to manifest. If the inquiry has been sincere, deep and persistent, it may be time for you to move to another approach. This one may have done its job and the work it can do at the present time for you is over. If this is the case, don't hang on to the old inquiry trying harder and harder to make it work; when the boat has taken you across the river, leave it at the beach and take the next step in your journey.

The next question or step quite likely will somehow mysteriously manifest. It may be another teacher, book, video, reading, question, or practice that reveals it. It will be apparent in the same way as was the current inquiry, by the feeling of "yes", of the knowing in your deepest self that this is the right, next step for you, now. In my experience, there is no greater confirmation of the path and your work than this mysterious appearance of the next key to the next door, out of nowhere. At times, it can be so amazing that it will bring you to tears, laughter, or just a smile or a head shake at the grace involved.

Watch for the difference between that knowing of the next step from your deepest self and just window shopping. One of the great pitfalls is to become a dilettante seeker running from workshop to workshop, teacher to teacher, or book to book as the search takes on an addictive quality. As the old metaphor goes, you only have so much time to find water, you can either dig 100 shallow wells or one deep one. You're more likely to find water with a deep well.

In your process of self-inquiry and discovery, as the reality of the mind and the I are seriously questioned, the mind will use every trick and resource at its disposal to attempt to derail the process. Whatever your most deeply held fears, attachments, memories, anxieties, fantasies, and hurts are, they will be eventually be brought into consciousness. This is not a game for the faint of heart. You are playing for all of the marbles and the I has its very existence at stake. As these great challenges emerge, welcome them, inquire into them, asking "Who has this thought or feeling?" or "Where did this come from?" The great challenges may emerge again and again. Ultimately, they will lose their strength and ability to entangle you.

Don't lose sight of the fact that enlightenment is about revealing that your real nature, your natural state is stillness, happiness and presence. It is not something you need to go out and manufacture or obtain; it is already there. All that you need to do is get the clouds out of the way.

If you get caught in a particular web of thoughts and are unable to break through, it may be helpful to use the questions from Byron Katie's books to disentangle or loosen that particular knot.

Do not get caught in the psychoanalysis of what events led to this challenge and whether it was due to your parents, schooling, genetics, lifestyle or economic situation. These are endless traps which allow the I to continue to be engaged, maintaining a dominant role, deciding what is right and wrong and what to do about it, all to avoid the day of reckoning. Ask yourself which I is going to decide which I is wrong and how it got that way and what to do about it? Who gets to lay out the path to improve the I?

Realize that traditional psychologists and psychiatrists will be of little help in pursuing enlightenment. Few know much about awakening and even fewer have personal experience with it. Simplistically, their approach is trying to fix the I and make it conform to some model that fits within certain behavioral ideals. Deconstructing the I and tossing it aside as a phantom in order to awaken is the completely opposite approach. For background on this disparity and possible negative outcomes of a classical psychological approach to awakening, read *Collision With The Infinite* by Suzanne Segal.

As Ramana says in *Who Am I?*, "Just as one who wants to throw away garbage has no need to analyze it and see what it is, so one who wants to know the Self has no need to count the number of categories or inquire into their characteristics…" (9)

H. Negations—How can saying you're not something be useful?

At the heart of realization is the knowing that all is One. An important step is apparently taken in exactly the other direction, to recognizing everything that you aren't. This disidentification, done step by step, loosens your closest held attachments and identifications. With that, the way is opened to deconstruct the identity of that which held these attachments, the I. With that deconstruction, the house of cards falls down, and all identification and attachment ceases, and all is seen clearly as One. Much easier said than done, but it works, and has for millennia.

To begin this disidentification, you systematically investigate every belief, relationship, emotion, sensation, body part, functioning, thought, etc. you have to see if you are that or if you are something different from it. As you investigate each of these elements, you will see that there is a subject that sees it as well as an object that is seen. A fundamental principle is that if you see or sense something, you can't be that. You clearly cannot be both subject and object, so you can reject that object as not being you.

While the practice can be done with whatever arises, Shankara, the Indian codifier of non-dualist philosophy, has provided a powerful template in his *Nirvana Shatakam*, which is presented in the "The Teachings" section. This text is a powerful tool for inquiry and awakening through the process of negation and has been used for this purpose for over 1200 years.

Going line by line, element by element, investigate these statements at your own pace, or go your own way, and see if you are really not the parts of your body, senses, and mind and are not your relationships, fears, emotions or attachments. You will feel the corollary question emerge along with the negation statement, "Is that true? Am I not that?" The real test is asking and feeling in your deepest space if this is your truth. The negation then becomes an inquiry. As a seemingly impossible or incredible statement is made regarding a closely held belief, your mind will recoil with resistance and questioning. This opens the way for deepening the inquiry, and loosening and ultimately discarding this attachment.

Too often, this "not this, not this" (neti, neti) approach is treated as a blind, rote recitation, almost like a mantra, that one hopes will eventually lead to the understanding that this is the truth. To bring energy, depth and immediacy to the approach, it is important to *feel* the question within the statement, the inquiry buried within the assertion. It can be helpful to end your negations with the parallel question such as "Am I really not this body?" to make the inquiry explicit and more penetrating.

An example of how to work with a negation.

As an example, as you work with a negation such as "I am not these ears or hearing", see if that is true. As you hear something, are you what you hear or are you a subject that hears something? If you are the subject that hears something, you must not be those ears or hearing which you sense as objects. While this is intellectually simple, do you feel it as your reality? If it doesn't feel true for you, if something is uncertain about that statement, even a subtle doubt, then it isn't yet a reality for you no matter how many times it is repeated.

Carry "I am not these ears or hearing" a step further by assuming that if that were true for you, how would that feel? What would it mean if it was true?

Investigate it with a parallel question, such as "Who hears?" See if there is someone doing the hearing. Watch sounds being processed, see an identification being formed, an image being created and perhaps a story forming. Are you the one hearing? Is it necessary for you to be there for hearing to happen?

Focus first on sounds that are neutral and unlikely to engage the emotions, like the ticking of a clock or the hum of a computer drive or fan. Then try more emotionally-charged sounds like a favorite song, words from a close friend or loved one, or your least favorite politician. Who is hearing this? Who is having these emotions and judgments? Where do these thoughts originate?

How you can look at the entire body this way.

To look at the entire body, piece by piece, it can be helpful for you to have a template for your investigation. One of the classical ways from yoga is to consider the body as being made of three different bodies of different energies and subtlety. These bodies are called the physical body, the astral body, and the causal body. These three bodies are constructed of five different sheaths or koshas. The five sheaths are the physical, the vital, the mental, the intellectual and the bliss(ful). The astral body is comprised of the vital, mental and intellectual sheaths; the other bodies have one sheath each, the obvious ones. There are of course Sanskrit names and walls of books on them, which you do not need to read as it will not be on the test (for those of you who are university students).

Consider first the physical body, and the physical sheath (Annamaya Kosha), the "pieces and parts" of the physical manifestation. Can all of this be objectified by the subject who you believe that you are? Are you your liver, your backbone, your skin, your hair, your left hand? While these are magnificent manifestations that perform useful functions, are they something that is experienced, something that is useful, perhaps like a car or a suit of clothes, but not something that you *are*?

What about the vital sheath (Pranamaya Kosha), the first sheath of the astral body? It is composed of the different energies in the body, the energy associated with breathing, eating, digesting, eliminating, moving, and circulating blood and fluids. As you see or sense each of these critical functional energies in operation, can you see them as objects being experienced by you, the subject? Are these amazing capacities, something that you experience, that happens to make it possible for the body to function, what you are?

Move next to a more subtle level, to the mental sheath (Manomaya Kosha) which is composed of the mind and its functions. Are you these observations, fantasies, emotions, memories, fears, and projections, or are you what sees them happening as they occur?

As you experience a statement like "I am Mary (or whoever) and I am afraid of _____", see how that feels. Shorten it to, "I am Mary and I am afraid"; how does that change the feeling? Then drop it down to "I am Mary" and feel that. Finally, how does just "I am" feel? What is most real? As the statement shortened, could you feel it becoming more intimate, coming into you? What most represents your deepest truth, your deepest intuition? Are you that fear, or are you what experienced these changes? Does "I am" feel different from you?

Investigate next the intellectual sheath (Vijnanamaya Kosha), the last sheath of the astral body, comprised of your intellect and ego/I, and in some models, your conditioning, genetics, culture, beliefs, and personality. Do you see these as something that moves into and out of consciousness affecting it as situations arise? Are they objects being seen by a subject?

As you did before, look at the statement, "I am Fred, and I am an American (or Indian, European, Mexican, etc.) whose grandparents came from _____ and I'm proud of that." Try the statement, but drop the "I'm proud of that", and then the "from _____" and then the "grandparents". How does that change the feeling of the statement? Does it move deeper and deeper, closer and closer to what you are? Are you these relationships and identities, or are you what is watching them?

Try the next step by dropping the "American", how does that feel? Try it one last time, but drop the "Fred" so that just "I am" remains. What has changed in the feeling of the statement? Which is the deepest, most basic feeling, the clearest statement? Which of these are you?

Finally, look at the bliss sheath (Anandamaya Kosha), or causal body, composed of your desires, what you do to satisfy those desires, and what you experience as pleasure. What happens after a pleasure has faded and you want to repeat it? Are you the operation of these desires, or can this process of desire arising, being fulfilled, and then falling away, only to be pursued again, occur with you as the witness watching the show?

Is the doer of these actions always there or does it arise for a particular desire on an ad-hoc basis? Are you the screen upon which the entire drama unfolds? What remains after each drama is over?

An example of how it all works.

Think about a great desire that you have, perhaps for the ultimate ice cream cone. (Feel free to substitute your own greatest desire, if isn't Rocky Road or Cherry Garcia.)

Be aware of the desire arising, filled with memories of the past pleasure of eating a wonderful ice cream cone, the flavors, how it melted on your tongue, the coolness and sweetness and how it ended the craving. This great memory was followed quickly by your desire to repeat that pleasure. Now you want another, even better ice cream cone, perhaps a different flavor, or a larger cone, or another brand, more expensive or exotic, one that you've seen in a magazine or on the web. This is the bliss sheath (Anandamaya Kosha) in operation.

Your intellect and ego/I come to the game, and decide how you will get that ice cream cone, how to find the money to buy it, and just how far you will go to get it (intellectual sheath/Vijnanamaya Kosha). You then remember where you've found the best ice cream in the past, and become frenzied and emotional as you think about it (mental sheath/Manomaya Kosha). Your hands, feet, voice, breathing, circulation, eating, swallowing, and digesting are then energized to get and eat the ice cream cone (vital sheath/Pranayama Kosha). Your body carries out the physical actions of getting and eating the ice cream cone (physical sheath/Annamaya Kosha). And then the process starts all over again, and again, and again.

Was there ever a time in this process where you were not a witness to the cascade of activities and forces at play? Were all of these emotions, actions and processes what you were or were you the subject that saw or felt them occurring? Was there an "I am", a witness there at every step? Which is most true and basic in this process, a subject who sees it occurring, a doer that carries it out, or an unchanging "I am"? Before, during and afterwards in the great ice cream caper, what was unchanging, real and everlasting?

You are not the activities and operations of these five koshas. You can see clearly that you are a subject watching these different objects and functions do their ice cream dance. Going deeper, can you see that you are the "I am", the unchanging consciousness, the screen upon which all, including the ego/I, the subject, occurs? You are That.

A model of the I to work with in negations

As you work your way through this "neti, neti" process of negating this, this and this, it may be helpful to consider, conceptually, just how your "I" might have been assembled. A model that many students have found useful is the way you might assemble a ball of "Post-It" notes.

As our lives progress, there are millions of experiences that occur. Some of these were captured and recorded, but the vast majority simply passed by and didn't "stick". If the ones that stuck were actually written on Post-It notes that would help you remember them clearly. It would also be useful to have them in different colors showing their category for easy sorting. There would be yellow Post-It notes dealing with school such as "good in math", "not good in history", "don't need to work on English", etc. There would be blue "Post-It" notes dealing with athletics such as "basketball is fun but not tall enough", "no good at soccer", "not fast enough for field hockey", etc. There would be other categories and colors of notes for things like dating, popularity, friends, work, appearance, intelligence, partners, etc. These would then be assembled as they arrived over the years in an accidental, serendipitous humble-jumble fashion into a ball of colored notes. Somehow, someone (who knows who) decided that all of these single experiences over all these years on all of these different colored Post-It notes made a coherent thing called an "I". That is just impossible. It's just a ball of ad-hoc, randomly selected Post-It notes assembled in a haphazard fashion from the millions of experiences that were available. There is just no rationale behind assuming that it is all one single color, one single entity with a single identity.

This "neti, neti" exercise gives us the vehicle to take that ball of Post-It notes apart, note by note, and see if there is really an "I" there.

What will happen in the process?

After negating everything that can be objectified as "not me", you are left with only the subject free of any attachments, possessions, emotions, body, senses or thoughts. Then extending your investigation into the subject, the observer itself, you find that there is no observer either. What then occurs is that the entire structure falls apart. Amazingly, it is then apparent that everything is That, everything is One.

Some philosophies state that it is not logical that understanding that you are not your body, thoughts, sensations, relationships, emotions, etc. and that you are not a concrete entity should result in realizing that everything is One. Logically it should just stop at "OK, the "I" is a construct. There is nothing to be attached to anything." Life would then move on effortlessly from there without the previous mental turmoil. It is not necessary, nor even reasonable, for it to be apparent that everything is One. But that is what happens.

Many folk resist the practice of negation as they feel it is depressing and nihilistic and fear that they will be left in a void, in nothingness and oblivion. In my experience, it is just the opposite. It is a liberating, affirming, and empowering process that results in a state that is full and complete beyond measure.

In *Nirvana Shatakam*, which is used as our fundamental negation text, Shankara ends each verse with a powerful affirmation that he is formless, blissful Consciousness and is one with God. Only by realizing what he is not has he been able to become One with God. Nirvana Shatakam is, at its root, a celebration by Shankara of his Realization and awakening to what he truly is.

Similarly Ramana Maharshi's *Upadesa Saram*, also in the "The Teachings" section at the end of the book, states in Verse 22 that you are not your body, senses, energy, or mind. This is followed immediately with "I am the One, Beingness". Additionally, Ramana describes in Verse 19 an approach to eliminating the "I" by inquiry into where it comes from, and describes the "I" falling away. This is followed in Verse 20 with the recognition that spontaneously present in its place is the Self which is "limitless, full, Beingness".

I. Using Affirmations

Another powerful, but often poorly understood practice is using affirmations. These have been used to such an extent in Western self-help and "positive thinking" regimens that they are often disparaged in serious spiritual practice. However, as some prominent non-dual teachers were previously employed in teaching and selling commercial, popular positive thinking courses, it is not surprising that these approaches are being applied here as well. There are also highly regarded non-dualistic teachers, like Robert Adams in Ramana's lineage, who are austere and clear in their non-dualistic teaching and who were strong advocates of affirmations as important practices in awakening.

There can be a tendency to confuse affirmations as being necessarily "in the affirmative" or what many regard as positive statements. However, the broader context is that these are statements that you are affirming, or stating, as real and true, and they are not necessarily only positive. You can also affirm negations.

Ramana Maharshi himself, the archetype of meditative inquiry, stressed the value of regular reading, study and repetition of extracts from the *Ribhu Gita* from the *Siva Rahasya*, a collection of 1924 verses that are primarily affirmations of the nature of Reality. As Annamalai Swami observed, "Bhagavan (Ramana) often said that we should read and study the *Ribhu Gita* regularly. In the *Ribhu Gita* it is said; 'That bhavana (mental attitude) 'I am not the body, I am not the mind, I am Brahman, I am everything' is to be repeated again and again until this becomes the natural state.' Bhagavan sat with us every day while we chanted extracts from the *Ribhu Gita....*". (10)

Some of the most widely used affirmations are:

a.   I am not this body, I am not these thoughts
b.   Nothing that I see is real
c.   Everything is consciousness/Bhahman/One
d.   Everything is perfect just as it is
e.   I was not born, I will not die
f.   I do not exist
g.   I am all that is
h.   Everything is within me
i.   I am Brahman/Siva/Self
j.   I am That, That I am
k.   I am

The process is to select one or more of these (less is more in this case) and repeat it on a daily basis, first thing in the morning and last thing at night. The selection should be something that feels and resonates, in a deep intuitive way, as the right one to work with at this particular time.

This approach can also be extended by picking a periodic event during the day, such as eating, going to work, answering the phone, all odd numbered hours on the hour, etc. and then doing the same affirmation, either silently or out loud as circumstances and inclinations occur. If you work with these diligently, the affirmation will take on a life of its own and will continue to operate at a deep level, whether you consciously voicing it or not.

This process may be easy to logically discount as mere parroting and brain washing. But it has amazing power if properly and diligently applied. The brain washing objection loses its impact when you realize that you are continuously bombarded with brain washing from the internet, TV, music, parents, teachers, visual media, friends, etc. endlessly trying to engage, manipulate or change you. It is a tribute to the power of the affirmations that they will work even with time allocated to them which is small compared to the time most of us spend processing opposing messages from a host of external sources.

For some insights into this process of working with an affirmation, I would strongly recommend that you read *The Way of A/The Pilgrim* and *The Pilgrim Continues His/The Way* also called *A Pilgrim Continues On His Way*. There are many different versions by different publishers and authors. This is one of the great classics from Eastern Christianity on the use of affirmations throughout your day and life.

You must work with the affirmations deeply and ponder them, not merely repeat them mindlessly. You will find that they contain within them the implicit questions of "Is this true?" "Does this make sense?" and "Do I really understand and realize this at the deepest levels or is my understanding just intellectual?" Continue the affirmations within your meditation practice by making the assertion and then sitting with it and feeling the reality or unreality of it.

Affirmations can be added to a meditative inquiry practice by using an affirmation like "I am". The "I" is sounded internally on the inhale, the "am" on the exhale. This grounding into your reality can relieve stress and break a cycle of obsessive thought. When a thought arises, evoke the meditative inquiry "To whom does this thought arise?" When stillness arises, abide in it with the sense of the "I am" and the inquiry as energies, tones in consciousness. If the energy becomes disturbed or agitated, then take up the affirmation "I am" again.

In working with "I am", it is useful for you to see what happens as you attach other things to it, like "I am Fred", "I am Fred and I am mad", then "I am Fred and I am mad because of what Mary said to me". You can also build this around whatever is currently running as a thought loop. Then simply observe, and sit with the changes in the energy in consciousness and the activity of the thoughts as you build the chain. Then reverse the process and watch the changes. Successively get rid of each added piece until you are left only with "I am", and abide there.

This approach can demonstrate the process that we go through countless times a day in unconsciously building thought loops that ensnare us. Watching the changes in consciousness as it is expanded and then reduced can move you into an understanding of the nature of thought. This understanding will then begin to dissolve the delusions that run, and confuse your life.

J. Surrender—Is it possible? Is it necessary?

Few aspects of spiritual practice are so misunderstood, unreasonably feared and shamelessly exploited as the concept and practice of surrender. It is the one concept that the folk that I work with have the most difficulty. It is almost always the last hurdle.

Particularly in the West, with a strong culture of winning and losing, success and failure, the prospect of surrender is anathema to most people. Even the mention of the term in some classes causes cringes, as experienced travelers on the spiritual path have seen how the concept has often been abused.

Many believe, or are taught, that surrender is the giving of your possessions, house, car, family, savings, income, etc. to the guru, teacher or leader. This is supposedly done so that one can be removed from these obligations and the responsibilities and problems associated with them and thereby find freedom and peace. Unfortunately, it is not that easy. Giving something away doesn't mean that you give up your attachment to it.

What often happens is that surrendering becomes a bargaining process in which you negotiate with your God, guru or leader for favors. It becomes a spiritual marketplace, a holy eBay. "I'll give You this, if I get that." Or "If I give You some of my salary or possessions, You will give me Heaven or Nirvana, a better birth next time or better 'in between' period before my next birth." This process is pervasive in religions as the buying and selling of indulgences was what drove Martin Luther to break away from Catholicism. Exploitation and manipulation occur. As someone else gives more and becomes more worthy than you, she may receive a nicer costume, a fancier title, special medal or better seating closer to the guru or leader. Institutions of all sorts, in order to perpetuate and grow, have become masters at appropriating others' possessions through this system of installed guilt and promised graduated rewards.

True surrender, which ultimately is essential to non-dualistic awakening, is not bargaining for the best return on your possessions. Rather, it is total surrender of all attachments to those possessions, including, and particularly, the "I" that has the attachments. As Ramana Maharshi says in *Upadesa Saram*:

30. Surrendering the "I" is the greatest spiritual practice and leads to Self Realization.

Many spiritual seekers, fascinated with the drama, excitement, and thrill of the search, spend great time, energy, and resources chasing ever more sublime and obscure experiences and knowledge. This approach, unfortunately, strengthens the ego, the very entity that is the cause of the problem and that will have to be removed if the search is to be successful. Those who have been around the spiritual block have seen seekers who have had a glimpse of enlightenment, or something, and now possess an ego without parallel or hope of removal.

On the other hand, many practitioners who were successful in the search had to come to the end where all approaches had been tried and all had failed. They finally reached such a point of despair and hopelessness that they totally surrendered as there was nothing else left to do. Only after they realized that they couldn't do it, they couldn't make enlightenment happen, did awakening occur. Realize that the "I" can't do it, that the "I" is the problem. Only by removing it by a complete surrender of its very existence, will true awakening occur. The "I" very much wants to be around for the coronation, which is actually its own funeral. Unfortunately, without diligent practice to understand and expose the source of the problems as the "I", it is virtually impossible to truly surrender it.

Logically, giving up the "I" is crucial if enlightenment is to occur. If awakening is beyond the mind, how can awakening take place unless the I, present in the thoughts that make up the mind, is surrendered, totally relinquished? As long as the I insists on being present for its own funeral celebration, there will not be a funeral.

There is the philosophical point that often arises as a sticking point: "Who surrenders the I? Doesn't there have to be a doer, an I of some sort to do the surrendering?" If surrender is regarded as what occurs when I give up my land to an invader, then yes, there is someone to do that surrendering, who feels the pain of that loss, and who remains afterwards. We are deeply conditioned, particularly in this culture, to resist that situation.

Surrendering in this case comes from a different space. This is more like the acceptance that occurs at death. It is over and the imaginary I is disintegrating, not that it had any choice in the matter. This acceptance results from the recognition and understanding of its own falsehood and unreality.

In the interest of full disclosure, my surrender needed someone who would take it away, like Valkyries or angels. Without a Valkyrie, the I would not die, even though it was very weak, terminal and on life support. As I had been strongly anti-guru, refusing to become anyone's disciple, the I remained in the ICU. It was only when Ramana Maharshi appeared on the scene that the I gave up and was absorbed in Ramana. As Ramana had left the body decades earlier, it is a great mystery why his presence was so palpable as to be what was surrendered to. There is no logical explanation for how it worked, but it did.

Is there some practice you can do to surrender?

In order to weaken the I, it is important to identify and surrender its attachments, as was done earlier. It is unlikely that you will be able to surrender everything at once, so some process of sequentially and methodically letting go of your attachments is necessary.

A powerful surrender practice is to use a chant, like "Krato smara krutham smara", which was described earlier, to surrender attachments. These attachments can be comprised of the five sheaths, or koshas, all of the elements described in *Nirvana Shatakam* or everything that you can identify yourself. The chant can be done while focusing on whatever attachment you selected to work with. It may be helpful to place the left hand on the Spiritual heart on the right side of your chest with your right hand extended, palm upward, in a surrendering gesture. As your attachment is brought into consciousness, it is surrendered. The surrender can be to a guru, the Void, a mentally envisioned fire, the sun, etc. as you are moved to do. It is whatever you can visualize as consuming your attachment.

Another powerful approach to surrender is to just say "yes" in your meditation, or at the end of each breath cycle when there is stillness and space before the next inhale or exhale. It is also effective to say "yes" when there is a difficult situation occurring, when you are experiencing pain or complex deep emotions. You can direct the "yes" to a spiritual figure, teacher or guru. You may not even be clear on what you are saying "yes" to, but it carries the feeling of "This is OK just as it is. I surrender to this situation. I accept this." The whole universe is just waiting for you to stop saying "no" and to stop resisting. All you need to do is say "yes" and accept things just as they are.

Intellectual or scientific understanding that might help you with surrender.

Another useful approach to facilitate surrendering the I for those who are intellectually or scientifically inclined is to understand a few seminal discoveries that have occurred.

The first of these was from studies done in 1983 by Benjamin Libet at the University of California at San Francisco. In these studies, Libet and his colleagues published what has been called "a profoundly influential paper on the source of human control." In these experiments, participants watched a clock and noted precisely when they decided to flex their wrist, as well as when the movement actually occurred. The participants reported having the intention to move about 200 milliseconds before movement actually began.

The readiness potential of the brain was measured by electrodes placed over the motor areas of the brain involved in controlling movements to determine when the brain had begun initiating the movement. By also recording the electrical activity of the muscles involved in the wrist movement, Libet determined precisely when muscle movement began.

The result was that the activity of the brain to initiate movement started about 550 milliseconds before the action began. However, the participants were only aware of the intention to move 200 milliseconds before it occurred. Therefore, the brain had initiated the movement about 350 milliseconds **before** the participant was even aware of having made a decision.

The actions that we do are already well in process before we receive any notice that they are in the process of occurring. They are underway before we have an opportunity to generate anything that looks like conscious intent of deciding to initiate a movement. An action is not the result of a conscious process that we have initiated, but rather is a **result** of brain processes that were initiated without our knowledge. This finding has major implications for issues of free will and what is the role of the I.

Some argue that there is the opportunity for you to veto the action in progress once you do find out that it is going to take place, even if you didn't make the decision to initiate the action. However, what would be the basis on which you might make that decision?

Our current science tells us that our thoughts, feelings and behavior are determined largely by our genetics, learning and environment. If you try to change yourself, your goals are determined by the same genetics, history and environment. What is possible is largely determined by what already is.

Similarly, if you look at how the I will choose which information you will focus on in the future, those choices will be made with your existing I, which you did not consciously put together. Whether or not you will intervene when you find out that something is in the process of happening is also predetermined.

Another useful approach comes from emerging mathematical techniques and discoveries. The branch of mathematics called complex systems theory, or chaos theory, is focused on complex, dynamic systems. It looks at the impact of small, seemingly insignificant changes on the behavior of large complex systems.

This approach sprang from a computer modeling experiment that a meteorologist was conducting to forecast the weather. While doing his experiments, to save time he restarted his huge program in the middle of a run with the same data, but left off some seemingly infinitesimal numbers in one parameter. Surprisingly, the result for the entire weather system changed dramatically. This discovery led to the common metaphor of a butterfly flapping its wings in some distant part of the world causing a hurricane in the Atlantic Ocean.

From this accident, an entire branch of mathematics and physics emerged that is finding great application in many facets of life. Although much of complex systems theory is beyond what we need here, there are some key results that are useful for our work:

a) Situations are less predictable the farther you get from the initial conditions. This means that predictions on complex systems undergoing change (our lives) are unreliable, and become more so as time passes.

b) All parts of the system affect, and are affected by, many other parts of the system in a complex web of cause and effect and feedback. Predictions based on linear logic (a > b > c) do not work as there are too many different interactions taking place for b and c that are unknowable.

c) Completely unpredictable results can emerge even if the original conditions are known in great detail.

d) We believe that the more that we know, the better we should be able to predict the outcomes of a decision. However, because of all of the interactions and feedback, huge amounts of knowledge are required that are impossible to collect and assemble in time for even one simple decision.

e) The human mind is a limited instrument designed to make decisions in simple situations using simple logic. Short-term memory can only hold about seven pieces of information at a time. That may be OK for dealing with saber-toothed tigers outside the cave, but it is inadequate for today's complex world. This inability of our minds to generate decisions in our world with any good track record gives us great discomfort, uncertainty and fear.

A common metaphor is of a leaf dropped in a rapidly flowing stream. In a simple logical world, the leaf progresses in a straight line downstream without incident. In the real world, however, the leaf will be subjected to eddies and currents, different obstructions, changes in wind and weather, sinking with time, waterfalls, etc. Even if two identical leaves (which don't exist) were started together, their paths would soon diverge significantly.

As our world is that complex, moving stream, why do we believe that the I, capable of only simple decisions about a predictable world, could possibly make correct decisions? How can this I have the importance assigned to it? Just what value does it really have?

Complex systems theory is now being applied to psychological systems. In *The Psychological Meaning of Chaos*, Masterpasqua and Perna describe how traditional views of equilibrium and stability are assumed to connote healthy mental states, while non-equilibrium and disorder are judged to be unhealthy. Their contrary approach is that the opposite may actually be more correct. They believe that psychological pain results when one becomes locked in a futile attempt at stability and equilibrium "in order to maintain an old way of knowing and to resist the inevitable emergent novelty woven into the process of living." (11)

They also conclude that what looks like a disordered state may actually be the best way to deal with a continuously restructuring self that is the result of the complexity of today's world.

If you consider the different paths that events can take in the course of our daily life in even simple events, like meeting friends for lunch, there are many opportunities for other results. Going to a restaurant can bring up many situations with different likelihoods. Will the car start? Will traffic be a problem? Is there construction? Will you get a cellphone call that will change your plans?

If any of these happen, then a series of other unexpected events cascade from that event. For example, if there is construction what might happen? Will you have to detour? How long will the delay be? Will it continue for next week's meeting? If you detour, can you take the 8th Street bypass? How late will you be? Will the others wait? What if Bob has a meeting?

These have happened to most of us and are out of our control. A simple graphic illustrates how such event trees, even with only two branches after each event, demonstrate how accurate prediction and control of our lives is impossible.

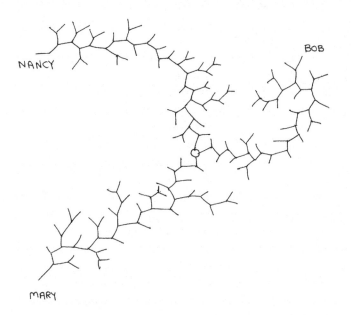

<u>*There are many possible alternative paths leading to any event*</u>

After a decision is made or an event occurs, our ability to predict all future outcomes of that event on all of the situations and people who will be affected three or four interactions by all of those people and situations is impossible to predict.

As another example, consider the game of chess. Imagine that the pieces represent the world. In this world, there are only two different families each with a father, mother, three sets of older twins and eight younger children. he movements that each can do is limited. Each "person" can only be in one of roughly 60 adjacent apartments. If a member of one family tries to move into an apartment occupied by a member of the other family, the only outcome possible is that the current occupant dies. Everyone moves around until one family is gone.

This is certainly a much simpler world than each of us occupies, let alone the entire population of the planet. However, the number of possible different sequences of interactions of those two families is calculated as 1 followed by 120 zeroes (about 1½ lines of zeroes). An estimate of the number of particles in the known universe is 1 followed by 70 zeroes. Do the math. Why do we believe that we can predict who and what will be affected by our interactions in our vastly more complex world?

What about trying to see scientifically if there is an "I"?

Our best scientists, using the most sophisticated techniques available, including high resolution electron and particle spectroscopy and microscopy, functional magnetic resonance imaging (fMRI), positron-emission tomography (PET), electroencephalographs (EEGs), cannot find an I anywhere. There is no homunculus, no little man sitting somewhere inside the brain running the show. There is not even one central point for all of the brain's activities.

The brain does not have one simple center of operations but many, many discrete centers dedicated to performing different tasks and functions. In many cases, communication between these functional centers may not occur or even be needed. What does jumping or tasting food have to do with solving math problems?

These dissociated ad-hoc areas developed as the brain evolved from species to species. Evolutionary anthropologists and biologists such as Jon H. Kaas have observed that as brains become larger they are larger mainly because they have added neurons. However, this larger size creates a problem. In order to connect these larger groups of neurons together, more and longer connections are needed. To keep the time for communication between neurons short, and to permit responses in a timely fashion so that we don't get eaten or whatever, it is necessary to have thicker connections. These thicker connections would mean that brains would need more and more of their precious mass devoted just to connecting neurons together.

It is found, however, that the brain does not simply add these connections in the number and size that would be needed to hook everything together into one entity. To solve this problem, the brain creates many modules to carry out certain specific tasks with short, local connections which are much faster and more efficient. The best known example is the two halves of the brain, which have different functional specializations to reduce the need for long connections for all tasks. As our scientists are discovering, there are over fifty different main areas in the human brain, with the neocortex itself probably having over 150 different regions devoted to different functionalities. Just where would the I be in all of these discrete regions?

As the scientists expand their tools to look at individual molecules, and then atomic entities and subatomic entities, at the end all is found to be space and energy. Using the principles of quantum physics, it is all energy waves and probabilities that something will form an apparent manifestation in some place at some time. There are no lasting, fixed entities anywhere. With the evolving approach using string theory as the basis for everything, the string elements which are envisioned are too small to ever be measured or identified. There just isn't an I anywhere.

Given these understandings, why is there a problem surrendering the concept of a central entity, an "I"? Why does this "I" construct have such power and control over your existence? Why is so much effort dedicated to make certain that this phantom is happy, fulfilled, satisfied, etc.?

Using what we know about the brain, how might this phantom "I" have been constructed?

Using what we know about the many discrete functional areas in the brain, and seeing that there is no central organizational point, what does this concept of an "I" mean and how is it structured? If the brain is a collection of associative networks grouped around functional areas, isn't it reasonable to assume that there are a host of ad-hoc "I"s?

These ad-hoc "I"s can be visualized as being equivalent to a series of Post-It notes created with associated content such as "My athletic skill is not that good", "I am a good daughter", "I have never been good in math", "I am taller than most of my friends", "I am ugly", etc. If we color-coded the notes as we discussed earlier, we could group them in the same way as the brain is organized. There would be a certain color for hearing, another for speaking, another for different physical and motor skills (athletics), another for learning language, etc. As we have seen, there is no link between these different areas. The structure is just a collage of different "I"s that occurs on an as-needed basis for different purposes.

As we know, there is a veritable blizzard of sensory impressions, experiences, inputs from others, pleasures, pains and fears which occur in our lives. From these millions, perhaps billions of possibilities, we are able to store only a tiny fraction. This selection of which snowflakes we will select from the blizzard and keep, as we can see from our daily life, is made haphazardly and accidentally. Another bunch of snowflakes could have just as easily been selected. These are then stuck together to construct our phantom "I", which we now know, is really a collage of "I"s.

As I lack the graphic skill to create a ball of these many functional areas, each with its own color-coded Post-It notes with appropriate messages, I have created a simpler model shown below which I hope will work for you.

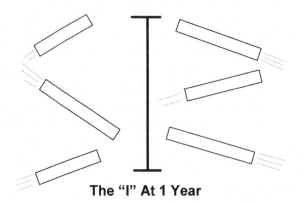

The "I" At 1 Year

Grandma's Sweetheart	Great Painter
	Daddy's Girl
Not Very Pretty	
Good At Math	
	Don't Share Well
Computer Wiz	
	Poor At Soccer
Bad Girl	Good Girl

The "I" At 8 Years

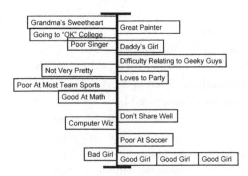

Grandma's Sweetheart	Great Painter
Going to "OK" College	
Poor Singer	Daddy's Girl
	Difficulty Relating to Geeky Guys
Not Very Pretty	Loves to Party
Poor At Most Team Sports	
Good At Math	
	Don't Share Well
Computer Wiz	
	Poor At Soccer
Bad Girl	Good Girl	Good Girl	Good Girl

The "I" At 18 Years

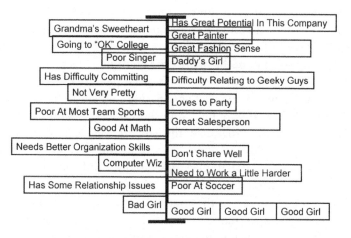

The "I" At 28 Years

How our "I" is built

The critical errors are in believing that the different-colored Post-It notes are true, that they have anything to do with one another, or that they somehow all fit together into one coherent whole. They are, after all, just collections of inputs of questionable accuracy randomly gathered on different subjects at different times by different functional areas of the brain.

Tremendous advances are occurring in the neuroscience of the mind/brain using a host of studies and tools. The phenomena of "neuroplasticity" (modification of the brain's functioning and structure resulting from experiences, training, or environment) which was believed to be impossible two decades ago, is now a scientifically-accepted fact. Google yields 29,000 hits. Whether it is chickadees constructing a new spring song, monkeys gathering food or humans using Braille, meditating or playing the violin, the results are consistent. Training enlarges the portion of the brain dedicated to those tasks. Additionally, if there are unused portions of the brain, like the visual cortex in the blind, they can be taken over by other functions like touch, hearing and even thinking.

Perhaps even more surprising is the discovery of "neurogenesis", or the creation of new neurons throughout life, also believed to be impossible. These new neurons are sent to the portion of the brain (dentate gyrus) believed to receive and sort information from the senses and which then decides where it should be sent. The new neurons can amount to 10 % of that section of the brain.

If you believe that you are your mind, and that your mind springs from your brain, and your brain is constantly being reconstructed and rebuilt, what does that say about the reality of an entity such as a personal "I/you?"

Understanding this science of the brain, can you begin to let go of the belief in this single entity, this "I", and realize that it is just a phantom? As this phantom "I" is triggered resulting in a thought, if you inquire "Where am I?" or "Who am I?" your thoughts will stop, if only for a very short interval. With this stopping, time after time after time, the structure of the network will begin to open up. The tightness of the linkages will begin to weaken. As the intervals between thoughts lengthen, the process will accelerate, perhaps rapidly, until that space becomes apparent, natural and continuous.

Surrender, or renunciation, is of the attachments of the "I" and finally, of the "I" itself. As Ramana Maharshi stated (in italics) in an exchange, "What is renunciation? *Giving up the ego.* Is it not giving up possessions? *The possessor, too.* The world will change if people will give up their possessions for the benefit of others. *First give yourself up and then think of the rest.*" (12)

K. Does it matter what you eat?

Ramana Maharshi, countless yogis and the *Bhagavad Gita* have all emphasized the importance of an appropriate diet for this work. It is stressed as a great aid to the practice of meditation, as certain foods can often result in energies that, depending on their nature, can slow or deaden, still or agitate the mind.

In the *Bhagavad Gita*, Chapter 17, verses 8–10 a useful categorization is offered which has been adopted in many yoga and meditation schools and modified and incorporated into many other programs.

Three categories of energies or modes of material nature are classically defined; sattva, tamas, and rajas. Sattva is categorized as being healthy, purifying, satisfying, free from attachment, and balanced and results in knowledge. Tamas is categorized as dullness, indolence, torpor, confusion and sleep and results in ignorance. Rajas is categorized as passionate, stimulating, craving and attachment and leads to activity, projects, cravings and restlessness resulting in suffering.

Sattvic foods are characterized as those that promote vitality, health, pleasure, strength, and long life. They are fresh, wholesome, firm, succulent and tasty. Examples are milk, butter, fruits, vegetables and grains.

Tamasic foods are overripe, stale, overcooked, tasteless, impure, rotten or prepared hours before they are eaten. Alcohol and "recreational" drugs fall into this category.

Rajasic foods are those that are energizing and promote passion. They are bitter, salty, sour, hot, harsh or pungent. Some examples are spices, meat, fish, eggs, and caffeine.

While these specific foods undoubtedly bear the mark of their cultural heritage, there is value in this perspective.

In one of my first yoga teachers' training courses, a well-known teacher approached diet and its effect on the mind in a very useful way. We were encouraged to maintain a journal on the effects that food had on the mind for a few weeks. In this log, you record what is eaten and what the activity of the mind is afterwards. If you eat spicy pizza and you become excited and agitated, then that is rajasic for you. If you eat oatmeal and a whole grain bran muffin and feel energized but calm, then that is sattvic for you.

General guidelines from a spiritual text or the latest diet craze are much less valuable than your own observations on what effect certain foods have on your emotions, energy and mental activity. You will probably find that some of the effects are different from what are generally given. You may also find that those effects change with time. As the Buddha said as one of his last statements, "Be a light unto yourself". That applies to the effect of food on your thoughts as well.

As your practice matures and deepens and your sensitivity and ability to watch the state of your mind increases, the effects often become more noticeable.

Changes may occur, so periodically repeating the food effects journal process can be very useful. You may also eventually find that which foods you eat has relatively little effect on the state of your mind.

Nevertheless, proper selection of what is for you, a mostly sattvic diet, can be a great aid in your practice. As Ramana Maharshi said in his classic *Who Am I?*, "Of all the restrictive rules, that relating to the taking of sattvic food in moderate quantities is the best; by observing that rule, the sattvic quality of mind will increase, and that will be helpful to Self Inquiry." (13)

L. Chakras

Work with the chakras, energy centers in the body roughly corresponding to bundles of nerves or plexes, and their energy source, called kundalini, has been used in this work by some folk. It was part of my practice at one point. Although this is not typically used in meditative inquiry, some practitioners have found it useful to work with these energies to remove blocks (vasanas) that may impede awakening. It is beyond the scope of this book to include extensive work in this area, and particularly here, a little knowledge is a dangerous thing. The works of Harish Johari and R.P. Kaushik can be very useful. Russill Paul also gives some excellent chanting work for the chakras.

My overall advice is to not get carried away with these practices as can easily happen. If these energies and their manifestations are meant to appear, they will, no matter what you try to make happen. You are not special or chosen if you have them, or forgotten or impaired in some way if you don't. Dance with them if they come and then let them go when they go.

M. Is there one simple practice to tie this all together?

The use of a simple chant of negation, inquiry and affirmation, coupled with the breath, can be a path that will embody all of these principles in a compact, accessible way. The chant is:

Vigraha naham, indriya naham, vrittiya naham, kutaham soham, kutaham soham

The last two lines can also be done *kutaham, kutaham* and *soham, soham, soham.*

This translates as:

Vigraha naham	-	this body	I am not
Indriya naham	-	these sensations	I am not
Vrittiya naham	-	these thoughts	I am not
Kutaham	-	where am I?	
So ham	-	I am That	

As we have done with earlier chants, each line of the chant, like "Vigraha naham" is done out loud on an exhale, followed either by silence or pondering the meaning or feeling of the line on the inhale. It can be very useful to focus your concentration into that region where that phenomenon is felt to occur: for sensations-in those senses, for thoughts-the head, for the body—throughout the body. During "Where am I?" bring the inquiry into consciousness as you feel the entire body, senses and mind. In "I Am That", focus the affirmation on the spiritual heart center to the right side of the chest, at the level of the physical heart.

This process can be done any time, and many times during your day, wherever you are, chanting mentally if that is appropriate, whenever it arises. Keeping this process going with a sense of watching and inquiring can have a powerful transforming effect.

N. What will awakening/Self-realization/enlightenment be like?

There is much confusion as to what you can expect after awakening. It is critical to remember that enlightenment is not an experience, no matter how ecstatic or sublime it might have been, nor how many you have had. If it has come and gone, it was an experience like so many others. In fact, an ecstatic spiritual experience may create such an intense longing for its regeneration, as it did in my case, that it becomes a great burden and an obstacle to true awakening.

In my case, the page turned totally unexpectedly while doing a yoga posture that had been done literally thousands of times before. I went into the posture one way, and came out of it completely transformed. There was no blinding flash of light, no choir of angels singing, no holding God's hand. Thought as a continuing phenomenon just stopped. The "I" was blown out like a candle in the wind. That has continued for what is now many years.

There are many who have a spiritual experience and declare themselves enlightened. You have probably heard "everyone is already enlightened", "a Buddha", and told to "call off the search". Unfortunately, that may not be your reality, but someone else's. Since you have never seen it before, it is easy to declare victory and leave the field prematurely. This leads to great confusion and the biggest loss of all, your losing the opportunity to make that wondrous mystery yours. If possible, have your enlightenment checked out by a bona fide Zen master rather than your buddies at Starbucks.

There are some useful markers that can serve as a guide. If awakening has occurred, there is no sense of anything further being needed, nor is there anything that can be taken away to improve it. Thoughts drop away as a continuing all-encompassing phenomenon in the foreground and fall to the background out of lack of interest. You move from being in a flock of birds to seeing a few birds far away in a clear sky. There is an ever present natural stillness, presence and deep quietness.

Thoughts, which are a lot like a sense, become more like taste-a useful tool employed when needed, rather than the constant hearing of a cacophony of jumbled noises. You no more force thought to stop forever than you would put out your eyes because you didn't like what you saw. It is an easy, comfortable state.

There is a knowing of a deep "yes"; of acceptance that you are not in charge, in fact that you are not. Rather than seeing that deep stillness as an observer, you dissolve in that deep stillness. You realize that you are that and have always been. There is an unshakable certainty, a knowing of completeness, fullness and limitlessness beyond any doubt.

There is also the knowing that this is nothing special, nothing special at all and that no one created it or has it as an achievement. There is the wonderment that it could have been overlooked for so long as it is so clear, intimate and simple.

Daily life continues in apparent duality through a personality, or persona, like an actor in a play simultaneously with a Oneness that is there continuously, naturally, easily. It is like one of those drawings that are two different things depending on your perspective, being either a vase or two people, or an older woman or a younger one. Or one of the current graphics that reveal the hidden picture within the apparent one after you stare at it for a while. A subtle shift occurs.

You do not lose functional competency even for highly complex tasks and positions. If that is what is going to be, you can continue in a complex job with a family, a mortgage, etc. In my experience, your functional competency will increase. Your full awareness will be present rather than the typical situation of having only a fraction available because it has to fight through a wall of constant thought. You will often be the only person there who can see from an unencumbered perspective what is going on. Solutions to complex problems in business situations and relationships will arise in consciousness; solutions that are beyond anything that you could ever have developed by thinking about them endlessly.

It is clear everything is within your consciousness, and that everything is One manifesting as apparent entities. If everything is One, then you as a discrete entity must not exist. Nisargadatta Maharaj's famous quote on this realization is "When I see that I am nothing that is wisdom. When I see that I am everything that is love. Between these two my life moves."

There is much discussion on whether anything changes after enlightenment and if there are degrees of enlightenment. Changes in the state of consciousness after awakening occurs are described by Ramana Maharshi, Nisargadatta Maharaj and many Zen folk including the contemporary Adyashanti. There are detailed descriptions within the Zen Buddhist tradition of various stages that occur after enlightenment.

A famous dialogue between a 20th century Zen master and his student address this issue. The student wrote "Truly I see that there are degrees of depths in enlightenment." The master replied "Yes, but few know this significant fact." Their discussion goes on to describe in classical Zen fashion and metaphors what those stages are. The Zen master states that "What these people (contemporary Zen teachers) fail to realize is that their enlightenment is capable of endless enlargement." (14) These are virtually the exact words used by Adyashanti, one of the clearest and most accurate contemporary teachers on what happens after awakening.

The prospect of endless enlargement of enlightenment begs the obvious question of who is doing such a process and who decides when it's over. If the process is clearly occurring without a doer, it is all just happening by itself, just as it is and there is no concern. If there is someone there who believes they have become enlightened and is now doing a process to be more enlightened, there is indeed further to go. In my own experience, these processes occur perfectly just by themselves and are different from anything that could have been predicted or imagined. It is all a total mystery, just as it has been all along, out of anyone's control, although it just wasn't realized.

Ramakrishna, the 19th Century Indian yogi, admonished students to "go further, go further". When in doubt, "go further". Search for your own deepest truth. At some level, you know in your deepest space if you are truly free and whether or not there is still something lacking. Be totally, brutally honest with yourself. There is no risk of "going past" enlightenment; there is a great loss in not going far enough.

There is a trap, however, in hearing all of this. The mind, anxious to grab hold of this threatening mystery, wants a model, a set of parameters and an idea of what it looks like, so that it can produce it and remain in control. It is impossible. No description is adequate because it uses the words and concepts of the mind, the source of the problem. Awakening is outside and beyond the mind. As long as there is a mind or an I trying to construct such a state with its tools, enlightenment cannot happen.

The Teachings

The three teachings presented here were chosen as I have found them to be the most useful, powerful and accessible. Teachings are useful to answer the question as to whether the author is perhaps just an imbalanced deluded soul, or if there is someone who is reputable who has had these same perceptions and understandings. It is also more credible if the teachings have all not just been gathered from the author's friends over the last few years.

These three teachings are from three different millennia, one within the last 100 years, another 1200 years ago and the third 2500 years ago. All three authors are generally accepted as being fully awakened. These teachers and these texts are three pillars of awakening.

I had originally included the Sanskrit Devanagri characters for each text, but it became too cumbersome and is probably of little or no value to most readers. If you do want the Devanagri text, it is in the texts in the Bibliography.

The transliterated Sanskrit, which gives English representations of the Sanskrit sounds, has been further simplified. (Unless you are "into" Sanskrit, you can skip the rest of this paragraph.) Palatal (P) and cerebral (C) sibilants are both "sh". No distinction is made between the guttural, P, C and dental (D) "n"s. No distinction is made between the C and D, aspirated or unaspirated, "t"s or "d"s. Anusvaara (nasalized preceding vowel) is indicated by an "M" and visarga (aspirated preceding vowel) by an "H".

In chanting the text, if you see a capital M or H, then make the preceding vowel sound more into your nasal cavity as an "m" for the M, and like a "haah" with more aspiration for the H. Sanskrit "a" sounds like the "u" in "but" or like "ah"; "c" like the "ch" in "chunk". Pronounce the Sanskrit "t", "d" and "n" with the tongue against the back of the teeth, making a "thah", "dhah" and "nhah" sound with a typical following "a". Pronounce "i" like in "it" or "ee"; "e" like the "a" in "play"; "u" like in "put". Double consonants like "aa" are twice as long with more aspiration, like "aah". If a "-" appears after a word, then that word is chanted together with the next one.

This is not perfect Sanskrit, but it will be about 92.36% correct, more or less. In my experience, it captures much of the power of the Sanskrit without moving past the point where many Western students are put off by it. Listening to someone else chant it is very helpful. If you want to learn Sanskrit, I would recommend the courses offered by Vyaas Houston at the American Sanskrit Institute.

A. *Upadesa Saram*—The Essence of the Teachings of Ramana Maharshi

The *Upadesa* (Teachings) *Saram* (Essence), or "Essence of the Teachings", of Ramana Maharshi is a comprehensive, practical guide to awakening to the reality that we are. It is a straightforward text given by Ramana Maharshi in response to a request from a poet wanting to conclude his rendition of a classical mythological story of Hinduism. As Ramana seldom wrote except in response to a question, this was a common device used by those around him to elicit his teaching.

The version produced here is from the Sanskrit, translated by Ramana Maharshi from the Telegu, which was translated from the Tamil, both south Indian languages, in which he originally gave it. This rendering into English is a synthesis of translations, interpretations and personal understandings. As such it is a free, rather than a strictly literal translation. If you want to hear what different chanting arrangements are used, a chanted version is available on the author's website at www.happiness-beyond-thought.com, as well as on the Ramana-Maharshi.org website.

I added the questions, their format, the discussions and the short poems following each verse in an attempt to make Ramana's teachings more accessible. Anything that works here is from Ramana, anything that doesn't is mine. However, neither of these folk ever really existed. Everything actually comes from nowhere.

1.

Can you obtain limitless freedom and stillness, a state beyond the mind, through your own actions?

kartur-		*aajnaya*	*praapyate*	*phalam*
of God		by the laws	obtained	result

karma	*kiM*	*paraM*		*karma*	*taj-*	*jadam*
action	is it	limitless		action	that	is inert

The ultimate outcome of actions is determined by the laws of the Universe. How can you hope to produce awakening by your actions?

All of the ultimate results of your actions are beyond your knowledge or control. How can you undertake an action believing that it will produce a given result, and only that result, when you have no ability to predict or determine its many outcomes? The results of your action, several interactions later, with unknown others in any of numerous side branches are unpredictable. The factors and energies in any situation are also the result of a multitude of intersecting chains of actions and reactions which are unknown to you. Given these limitations, it is even more unlikely that the actions that your mind could come up with could produce a state that is limitless and beyond the scope of the mind.

How can I decide what to do?
Where did these choices come from?
How will they all finally work out?
How will everyone else be affected?
Things never turn out how I expected
I'm just not in control.

<u>*2.*</u>

<u>*What happens if your actions are focused totally on what you want?*</u>

kriti-	*mahodadhau*	*patana-*	*kaaranam*
of action	vast ocean	fall	cause for

phalam-	*ashaashvataM*	*gati-*	*nirodhakam*
result	limited	liberation	obstruction

If you undertake actions with a goal, the result will almost always not be what you intended. The result will be better or worse, so it will lead you to more actions and frustration and will block your progress towards liberation.

Actions that you take with the intention of producing a specific outcome, given your inability to control and predict the outcomes, gives you a result that is normally not what you intended. Normally it will be less than what you had hoped, and different in some aspects even within what you can see immediately. Also, there will be many unintended and initially unknown consequences for others and for you. These failures will lead you to perform other actions to remedy the shortcomings of the first attempt, causing you to "fall into a vast ocean" of further actions. These actions will similarly produce frustration, unhappiness and disappointment. Operating in this doomed manner, you are unable to find a way to achieve lasting satisfaction and happiness.

It didn't quite work out last time like I'd hoped
And I had no idea it would affect them that way.
This time it will be different
A different approach and I'll try really hard
Oh no! Not again!
Now what do I do?

3.

How should you look on the results that are obtained from your actions?

iishvara- god	arpetam dedicated to	necchayaa not out of desire	krtam done
citta- mind	shodhakaM purifies	mukti- liberation	saadhakam means

If you surrender your attachment to the results of your actions, that will purify your mind and provide a path to liberation.

Rather than performing actions focused on achieving something that you want, perform actions as they arise with no attachment to the outcome. Remain open to whatever occurs instead of operating with the sense of you as a doer who will succeed or fail. This will loosen the grip of your mind and open the way to freedom.

I give up!
I can't make things happen like I want.
I'm totally caught up in what happens.
What if I just do what I can with whatever comes up
And let whatever happens be OK, whatever it is?
It has to be OK.
That is what happened after all.

<u>4.</u>

<u>*What relative priority should you give to different spiritual practices?*</u>

kaaya-	*vaan-*	*manaH-*	*kaaryam-*	*uttamam*
physical	oral	mental	action	most beneficial

puujanaM	*japash-*	*cintanaM*	*kramaat*
physical worship	chanting	meditating	respectively

In selecting your spiritual practices, realize that the most powerful approach is meditation; chanting is less effective and physical actions like rituals are the least effective.

Your most important actions to obtain liberation and freedom are mental ones, like meditation, as the mind is the main obstacle and the source of your problems. Verbal practices, called japa, like chanting or mantras are less direct and less likely to affect the mind. Physical actions like rituals, or pujanams, are the least direct and are even less likely to solve the problems caused by the mind.

Ceremony, chanting, meditating
Which is closest to the bone?
Mind is the root of the problem
All paths may ultimately get there
But why not take the direct route?
Meditate on it.

5.

How should you do your physical practice?

jagata	iisha-	dhi-	yukta-	sevanam
the world	God	attitude	accompanied with	serving

asta	muurti- bhrd-	deva-	puujanam	
eight	forms	God	physical worship	

Rituals should be done with the attitude that you are serving the world, which is God.

You should practice physical worship, or pujanam, with the attitude that you are serving the entire world, in all its aspects, forms and entities and that it is in reality all One, or God. This includes earth, water, fire, air, ether, sun, all celestial bodies, and all conscious beings. When you do this physical worship, whether it is with a statue, icon, natural object, picture, or photo, what you are worshipping is not that article itself, but the Oneness of it is a part.

This photo, this statue, this picture,
The sun, your finger, the birds,
The trees, the virus, the sea,
The beloved, the insects, the whales
The scorned, the Milky Way, and you
All, all, all are God

6.

How should you do your verbal practice?

uttama-	*stavaad-*	*ucca-*	*mandataH*
of the Lord	praising	chanting aloud	low murmuring

cittajaM	*japa-*	*dhyaanam-*	*uttaman*
mental	chanting	meditation	most effective

Of all of the ways that verbal worship can be done, mental chanting as a meditation is the most effective.

You can perform verbal worship by chanting out loud, murmuring or whispering, or internally in the form of a meditation. Of these, the internal mental chanting is the most effective as it is closest to the source, the deep stillness within and to the problem, the chattering mind.

> *I wonder if God can hear me*
> *Should I shout at Her, or just tell Her in a normal voice?*
> *What if I just whisper it?*
> *How do I get Her attention?*
> *Deeper, deeper inside is where She lives*
> *Deeper, deeper inside is where She'll hear me*

Z.

How should you meditate?

aajya-	*dhaarayaa*	*srotasaa*	*samam*
ghee	the flow	the flow of water	like

sarala	*cintanaM*	*viralataH*	*param*
unbroken	meditation	interrupted meditation	better than

Unbroken meditation, like water flowing in a stream or oil pouring, is the most effective.

When you meditate, you do it continuously, like the pouring of oil or the flowing of a stream of water. Meditation should not be limited to a set time following a prescribed procedure and then put away for later. Continuous meditation will lead finally to absorption in the process.

The metaphors for meditation of oil flowing and a stream of water are classical ones going back thousands of years. The oil that is flowing is ghee, or clarified butter used in lamps, cooking and spiritual ceremonies. It is thick and viscous, with a self-stickiness in which its various parts hold together. Like this, your meditation should have stickiness, a tendency to bind together with you like love rather than the scattered, disconnected assemblage your normal thinking is.

The flow of a stream of water captures the concept of uninterrupted, unceasing desire to reach the goal. A stream is not dissuaded in its drive to reach the ocean, continuing on past rocks, rapids, pools, falls, and even dams. It has an unstoppable desire to reach the ocean. When it reaches its goal, it then dissolves completely, unrecognizable and inseparable. With your meditation, the stream of thoughts, which you call "I," is finally absorbed totally in the Self, the ocean of bliss.

Meditate now or later?
Where should I sit?
Use a cushion or a chair?
Always, river to ocean flowing, oil pouring
Twenty-four/seven
Continuously, on, on, going on
Never not, naturally

8.

How should you meditate? What should you focus on?

| *bhedabhaavanaat-* | | *so-* | *ham-* | *it-* | *yasau* |
| better than a dualistic approach | | That | am I | thus | this |

| *bhaavana-* | *abhidaa* | *paavani* | *maata* |
| vision | nondual | purifying | the scriptural view |

Instead of meditating on an object, know that you are That, the One.

Rather than being an "I" meditating on an object to get a wonderful vision or a sublime experience, meditate on your being That, "I am", awareness itself. Meditate on what the Christian Bible says in Exodus, "I Am That I Am". Inquire into who is meditating, what this "I" is which is the source of your thoughts and problems. Then you can see your concept of the doer fade away and realize that awareness that is your true nature, the Self.

Meditating, an "I" on a "that" to get THE prize
Another search for more, and more, and more
End that search and become THAT
That "I am"
THAT I AM
I AM THAT

9.

What final state will you achieve in your meditation?

bhaava-	*shuunya-*	*sad- bhaavasusthitiH*
contemplation	free from duality	abidance in one's Self

bhaavanaa-	*balaad-*	*bhakti-*	*ruttamaa*
contemplation	the strength	devotion	best

The strength of concentration to abide as That is brought about by devoted practice.

The most effective meditation is abiding effortlessly in the awareness that you are. There is no meditator, anything to meditate upon or any hoped-for result. Devotion to the practice enables you to rest in that natural stillness of the Self, free from duality.

Absorbed, absorbed, absorbed
Beyond someone being in, or with, or having, anything
Beyond a doer doing something to get somewhere
Empty, no one,
Nothing
Just This, just This, just This

10.

Where should you direct the focus of your meditation?

hrtsthale		*manas-*	*svasthataa*	*kriyaa*
in the heart		mind	abiding	action

bhakti-	*yoga-*	*bodhaash-*	*ca*	*nishcitam*
devotion	yoga	knowledge	and	the view of the scriptures

If the mind is absorbed in the Heart, all spiritual practices are accomplished.

If your mind is absorbed in the spiritual heart, this will accomplish all that you can gain through your spiritual practices, including rituals, mantras, chanting, yoga, devotion and spiritual knowledge. Your spiritual heart is on the right side of your chest, the point that everyone touches when they say "I did that". This spiritual heart is often identified with a separate chakra called the "hridaya" which is associated with the heart chakra (Anahata). It is discussed in Johari's *Chakras* and in *The Serpent Power* by Sir John Woodroffe. Your meditation should be focused there rather than on the traditional dualistic meditation focal points such as the third eye, the navel center (hara), tip of the nose, palm of the hand, chakras or energy centers.

Navel, chakras, third eye, tip of the nose
Where to focus my meditation?
Here, just here, absorb your mind back into your Heart
Be done with practices and learning
Be done with praying and rituals
Be done with it all
Forever

11.

How can you calm your restless mind so that you can meditate?

vaayu-	rodhanaal-	liyate	manaH
breathing	by restraining	is absorbed	the mind

jaala-	pakshivad-	rodha-	saadhanam
in a net	like a bird	for controlling	a means

Control the breath and you control the mind, like throwing a net over a wild parrot.

If your mind is racing wildly, focus your attention on your breath. Slow and deepen your breathing and your mind will also be slowed, perhaps stilled. Remain conscious of your breath after your mind slows and you will be able to retain that stilled mind. Visualize this controlling of the mind through controlling the breath as if you were throwing a net over an excited bird or grabbing the reins of a chariot being pulled by wild horses.

Wild, monkey mind
Jumping branch to branch
Screeching frenzied parrot
Flapping crazily
Caught, stilled, netted
Breath stilled, mind netted
Monkey, parrot, asleep, quiet
Still

12.

How does slowing the breath slow the mind?

citta-	vaayavash-	cit-	kriyaa-	yutaaH
mind	functional energies	consciousness	activity	are linked

shaakhayoh-	dvayii-	shakti-	muulakaa
branches	two	one power	root cause

Mind and breath, consciousness and action, are joined like two branches on a tree, both with the same root ...

The mind and the energies of breathing, digestion, circulation, etc. are linked to consciousness and activity. By controlling one, the others are controlled. If your breath and your energies are calmed, your mind will be calm and present and your activities will be efficient and focused. Similarly, if your mind is calmed and still, your activities and breath will be calm and focused.

Thought, doing
Mind, breathing
Nearby branches, one trunk
One tree, one root, one energy
Still one
Still all

_13._

**Once you've calmed your mind, is that what you're aiming for?**

laya-	vinaashane	ubhaya-	rodhane
submergence	destruction	two	forms of control

laya-	gataM	punar-	bhavati	no	mrtam
submergence	attained	again	is born	not	dead

Calming of the mind can be either temporary or permanent. Lasting calm can only be attained if the mind is restructured and absorbed.

There are two different approaches to control the mind: a) do some activity or process to temporarily suppress the mind or b) bring about a total restructuring of the mind that dramatically and permanently changes its functioning.

In the first approach, your mind can be lost temporarily in some activity like rock-climbing, sex, chess, surfing, dancing, playing a video game, watching a movie, etc. It can also be brought about through spiritual practices like chanting, breath control, yoga, rituals, etc. It is also possible to get peak experiences in these activities, which, as we all know, are very seductive.

Unfortunately, when the activity stops, the mind quickly reemerges and takes up where it left off. Thoughts come up like "That was great? How can I do that again?" The state is only passing through and will soon demand a repeat performance at an even higher intensity. This is "Not it."

In the second approach, the structure and operation of your mind is permanently changed. The "I" leaves center stage and plays a minor role, much like your senses. There is a permanent stillness with great clarity, energy, and a joyful, peaceful awareness. There is no feeling of there being something missing that could be added to improve it, or of it being possible to remove something to make it better. Thoughts fall away naturally out of lack of interest.

This restructuring of the mind or "I" does not make you non-functional, a common fear. On the contrary, a functional "i" remains which performs with higher capability. Tasks are accomplished as they emerge without attachment, fear or concern. Because the scattered, random, ceaseless thoughts, biases and agendas that previously filled your consciousness are gone, you are often the only person in the room who shows up 100%. You look like a genius because everyone else is only 15 % present. This is "It."

Not it

Mind, thoughts lost in the action
This is great! I've done it!
Oh no, #*&#*!, it's gone!
Where did it go?
How did I do that?
What do I have to do to get it again?
Action, more action, more action

It

Just quiet
Peace, still, clear, easy
Nowhere to go
Nothing to be added or taken away
No edges, no boundary
Just THIS
Empty fullness, full emptiness
THIS

_14._

How do you obtain that restructuring and absorption?

| praana- | bandhanaal- | liina- | | maanasam |
| breathing | controlling | absorbed | | mind |

| eka- | cintanaan- | naasham- | ety- | adaH |
| the One | contemplating | destruction | gains | that |

Lasting absorption of the mind can be accomplished by first stilling it through breath control, and from that state, contemplating That.

After you calm your mind through control of your breath, instead of hanging out in that state, which will prove to be temporary, use this as a window to go deeper. From that calm state, inquire "Who hears?", "Where am I?", or "What is this?" Or, use an affirmation like "I am not this body, not this mind. I am That, I am everything." Moving from stillness into inquiry, you may come upon what is behind it and your mind, and you, will be absorbed. You will realize that awareness and presence that is your true nature, what you really are, your true Self.

Breathing, watching, thoughts slow, stop
Empty fullness, what is it?
Where am "I" in this emptiness?
Inquiring, inquiring, on and on
Suddenly, unexpectedly,
Nothing and everything

15.

Once you are abiding in the Self, is there anything else to be done?

nashta-	maanas-	otkrshta-	yoginaH
lost	mind	exalted	yogi

krtyam-	asti	kiM	sva-	sthitiM	yataH
to be done	is there	anything	own nature	abidance	attained

If your mind becomes absorbed, there is nothing else to be done.

When your mind and "I" become absorbed in your true nature, your Self, you will realize that there is nothing else to be done. You will be in a state that is unique, yet present everywhere. It will be clear that there is nothing that you could do to make it better; it is complete and perfect. There is nothing to be done, nor is there anyone there to do it, nor was there ever anyone there.

Sitting quietly
Full of nothing
Complete, no adds or take-aways needed or possible
How could there be something to do?
And who would do it?
There never was anyone there.

_16._

What else can support this process of absorption?

drshya-	_vaaritaM_	_cittam-_	_aatmanaH_
perception	withdrawn	mind	one's

cittva-	_darshanaM_	_tattva-_	_darshanam_
awareness	recognition	Truth	recognition

Withdraw your mind from your perceptions and recognize your Truth.

If you withdraw your attention from the messages that come from your senses and follow their path back into the analyzer of those sensations, and then further back into what it is that watches this process, your will be at your true Self. There you will recognize that this stillness, this awareness within which all sensory perceptions, and all thoughts, unfold, is your True Nature.

I always wanted one of those in the window
I always wanted one of those
I always wanted one
I always wanted
I always
_I . . . ._

17.

What is your mind, how is it constructed and how does it operate?

maanasaM	tu	kiM	maargane	krte
mind	what is		inquiry	is undertaken

na-	iva	maanasaM	maarga	aarjavaat
not	indeed	mind	inquiry	most direct

If you search for your mind, you will find that it doesn't exist.

Looking with great curiosity and openness at your mind in the same way you look at a new person, city, or food, you will find that there is no such entity as a "mind". Look from all angles, at different times, and under different situations, always seeing if you have such a thing. What color is your mind, what does it feel like, what is its energy, how big is it and where does it live?

We believe that there is a single entity called the "body". In reality, your body is a conglomeration of made-up entities with names like eyes, nose, fingers, tongue, teeth, stomach, intestines, blood, and cells. Because it moves around as a single unit from place to place, we believe that it is a single entity. When the time comes to deal with an acute illness, however, we direct the treatment to the part where the problem lies. Looking deeper into each apparent sub-assembly, we find it made up of smaller and smaller entities, and eventually just a mass of a huge number of cells, fluids, and strange disconnected particles of all types.

Similarly, we treat our car as a single entity, as it also moves as one piece (most of the time). We recognize, however, that it is an assemblage of tires, pistons, valves, doors, seats, windows, motors, etc. When it stops moving (other than in traffic), the search begins for the individual component that failed and we attempt to repair it so the apparent conglomeration can move again. Again, at the deepest level, it is just atoms, energy and space.

"Mind" is just a convenient term assigned to something that is really an aggregation of pieces. If you analyze carefully what the mind is, it is just a continually changing array of unrelated strings of thoughts. It is just thoughts.

As Thich Nhat Hahn has observed, a piece of paper is not made from "paper", but from many different strands of "non-paper"; mind is likewise only an apparent reality made from thoughts.

Do I have a mind?
Where is it?
Can you bring it to me?
Can you have it all show up at once?
Who decided what it would contain?
Does anything tie it all together?
Or is it just raindrops being called a storm?
Never mind
Never a mind.

<u>*18.*</u>

<u>*If there is no mind, how are thoughts organized and structured?*</u>

vrttayas-	*tv-*	*ahaM*	*vrttim-*	*aashritaaH*
thought forms	but	I	thought	dependent upon

vrttayo	*mano*	*viddhya-*	*ahaM*	*manaH*
thought forms	mind	know	ego	mind

Your mind is nothing but thoughts based on an I.

Looking carefully with curiosity and openness, you have seen that the mind is only an apparent reality, just thought streams that you have tried to glue together into an entity. Now, look at the thoughts themselves to see if there is any common trait, any characteristic that might lead to understanding their structure.

As you watch your thoughts carefully for a few minutes, put them into two buckets. (Mental buckets of course.) One bucket contains thoughts with an "I, me, or mine", either implicitly or explicitly buried within them. The other bucket contains thoughts without any hint of an "I". What do you discover?

Virtually everyone will find that the vast majority of thoughts are not sensations or information, but contain an "I", obviously or in some second-hand way, in some form.

This recognition that most thoughts have an "I" as their basis is the door to an approach that makes it possible to unravel the structure and foundation of thought and to end its tyranny.

Endless thoughts, pebbles in a stream
Every pebble-a different shape and size
Every pebble made of stone
Every thought—a different shape and size
Every thought made of "I"

19.

Using this understanding that thoughts contain an "I", how do you use that to be free?

aham-	ayaM	kuto	bhavati	cinvataH
I	this	where	arises	one who inquires

ayi	pataty-		ahaM		nijavicaaranam
oh	drops		I		self inquiry

See where the I comes from and it will disappear.

Knowing that your thoughts are constructed around an "I", look for where that "I" is. Where does this I come from? Where is it right now? Keep asking, perhaps shifting to saying "I, I, I", and watching where it arises. Look for its source and see if it has a permanent location and existence. Does it arise each time in each situation?

Similarly, silently repeat your name. Feel the energy that comes with that sound, feeling the space before it arises, as it is there, and as it passes away. With curiosity and openness, watch this process. What causes this gathering together into an identity? Is this real? Does it constantly exist, or does it come into being each time? What is associated with or attached to this identity?

Carefully answering these questions, and seeing its unreality, the I falls away.

"I", "I", "I", "I"
Where do you come?
Parading around so self-important
Directing, discussing, regretting, planning
Wanting, needing, forgetting, complaining
Who created you?
Who put you in charge?
And just where are you anyway?

20.

What happens if this "I" falls away? What appears in its place?

ahami	*naashabhaajy-*	*aham*	*ahantayaa*
I thought	is destroyed	I,I, ...	

sphurati	*hrt-*	*svayaM*	*parama-*	*puurna-*	*sat*
shines	as Self	by Itself	limitless	full	beingness

When the I disappears, limitless Awareness is there.

When you realize that the I is a mere phantom, it loses its grip and falls away, but it is not replaced with oblivion or blank nothingness. This is the great fear that the I uses to sustain its apparent identity and maintain apparent control. What does appear wonderfully and instantly in its place is a pregnant presence, limitless and complete that has always been there, always.

In this process, you may experience periods of disorientation and uncertainty while this new reality is adapted to and integrated. This disorientation will weaken and pass as you realize that you don't know what is going to happen, but whatever it is, it will be OK and just as it should be. This limitless, full presence is always there, as it is what you have always been. It is not going anywhere. It cannot leave you, as it is you.

"I" gone—off somewhere
Full emptiness
Empty fullness
Nothingness and everythingness at once
Already there
Shining alone
No place for it to go

21.

Is there any daily experience that gives you more insight into this "I"?

idam-	*ahaM*	*pada-*	*abhikhyam-*	*anvaham*
this	I	word	that is called	daily

ahami	*liinake*	*apy*	*alayasattayaa*
I thought	is resolved	even	destruction-free existence

Every night in sleep, the I disappears and there is peace.

Every night, when you fall into deep sleep, the I disappears and there is peaceful abidance in your real Self. Only when awake, or in dreams, is there an I as the focal point surrounded by objects, emotions, problems, fears and situations.

Although few learn how to be aware of consciousness in dreamless sleep, it is possible. Whether or not you are aware of it, you must have a continuous consciousness. If you didn't, you would have to relearn existence each morning.

You can see this awareness without an I if, when you first wake up, before your world starts up, you are present for the deep stillness without thought, intention or necessity, just the presence that is there. This presence will be fleeting, so watch as your day begins, thoughts crowd in, and the stillness and presence is obscured. This same presence is there just before you fall asleep. Unfortunately, most of us are so tired that we pass through it without noticing. It is much easier to see it in the morning when your energy is high. To set this up for tomorrow morning, remind yourself before you go to sleep to be alert for that presence the next morning. If you miss it tomorrow, then remind yourself tomorrow night. Eventually, you will see it. It is there, always.

You can experience this presence while you are awake by simply watching your breath carefully. Watch where the inhalation goes to and where the exhalation comes from, and where the exhalation goes to and the inhalation comes from. There is a space there, and watching it you will find the presence that is always there.

You can also glimpse this stillness by looking for the space between two thoughts or between two notes of music. As one thought or note ends and before the next one begins, watch that space. Where did the last one go and where did this one come from? It is the same stillness, the same presence that is always there.

Awake, "I am this, I am that, … "
Dreaming, "I am this, I am that, … "
Deep asleep, "Am I?"
Awake again, "Ah yes, here I am."
But who remembered?
And where did she come from?

Between breaths,
Between thoughts,
Between notes in a song,
What is there?
And where is she?

22.

What are you? Are you your body, senses or mind?

vigrah- body		indriya- sense organs		prana- energies		dhii- mind		tamaH ignorance

na- am not	aham- I	eka- One	sat Beingness	taj- that	jadaM inert	hy- therefore	asat unreal

You are not your body, senses, energies or mind; they have no voice, no beingness in themselves. You are the Beingness within which they occur.

Looking at the body, the senses, the energies that activate and maintain the body, and the functioning of the mind, you realize that they are all objects illuminated as they are brought into consciousness by a witnessing subject. They are inherently different from that aware witness. Only the witness is unchanging.

If you see a car passing by, you realize that you cannot be both the person who sees the car and the car. You cannot be both your elbow and the one who sees your elbow. They are different. Realizing that all objects are changing and are not you, you remain as the unchanging witness. Your attachment to those changing tools and capabilities through which functioning or sensation occurs weakens and falls away. The structure of your identity changes as you remain as just this witness.

Surprisingly, you then see that the body, senses, mind, and everything else is within you. I did not expect beforehand that it would be this way, but that is what is. It then occurs that if everything is within you, you must be every thing, so you must be nothing, and everything must be One.

Seeing
Body, senses, energy, mind
The unchanging witness that sees them
Cannot be these changelings
They are not you but somehow are within you
And you are everything
So you cannot be any thing
So you are nothing
And everything is One

23.

Is there a source for awareness? Is there something before beingness?

sattva-	*bhaasikaa*	*cit*	*kva ve-*	*taraa*
existence	illumines	consciousness	where is	another

sattayaa	*hi*	*cit*	*cittayaa*	*hy-*	*aham*
form of existence	thus	consciousness	form of awareness	thus	I

Existence is consciousness is awareness.

Is there some other consciousness that produces your beingness, awareness, your presence? Looking with great curiosity and integrity, you do not find another source for beingness. Consciousness, awareness and beingness are all the same. It is your fundamental, basic experience, your true nature.

Follow the path back to see what the steps are. Start with a sentence, such as "I am Fred and I am angry at Mary for what she said yesterday". Eliminate it piece by piece. Move from "I am Fred and I am angry" to "I am Fred" and then to "I am". Feel the different energies around these statements as they change.

From here, see if you can move beyond "I am" to just "I" or "am". Are they before "I am", or are they after it? Can you move beyond "I am" to a state that contains no sense of that condensation, to just "awaring"? Is there anything beyond this? How would you find it? Who would find it? Who would be there to describe it? Could it be described without leaving that state?

The terminology to describe these states varies in different traditions and with different teachers. Libraries are filled with discussions and descriptions of Universal Consciousness, Ground of All Being, Atma, Brahman, Parabrahman, different samadhis, levels of kenshos, etc. An ultimate state that is really beyond the mind cannot be cognized or accurately described by the mind. If you are concerned about what particular level or state you have reached, there is more to occur. Being just this, there is nothing to describe, and no one to describe it.

What lights up this watching?
What creates presence, beingness?
Is there something else behind, beyond?
Something before "I am"?
Peeling away the onion,

Layer by layer
Until the onion is gone,
Then only This, only This
What could be there to describe it?
Could it be described without rebuilding the onion?

24.

How are you different from God, the fundamental Reality?

iisha-	*jiivayor-*	*vesha-*	*dhii-*	*bhidaa*
god	individual	costume	attitude	division

sat-	*svabhaavato*	*vastu*	*kevalam*
beingness	essential nature	truth	only one

You and God are One, only your appearance is different.

The distinction between you and God is only an apparent difference. It is brought about by the appearance, or costume, that you and God have taken. Beingness, or God, and your own essential nature are at root exactly the same thing.

The statement that "everything is One" is not an imponderable abstraction to justify a philosophical belief. It is not just a scientific conclusion based on the latest physics and mathematics (although it is heading that direction), or some hoped-for situation brought about by decades of meditation in a cave. You can experience, here and now, in your daily life, the reality that everything is God.

I was standing at a counter in a market and it was clear, as crystal clear as anything can be that everything that was there, fish, carts, people, crackers, tile, counters, glass, olives, everything, was one, all the same, the same. Calling it "God", or "One", or calling something "God" and something else "everything" misses the reality. It is beyond concept. Mind desperately wants to bring it to a level that it could put into a box, categorize and own, but it cannot hit the mark.

This occurs often. Everything has an unreality to it, a non-fixity to its edges and form that confirms oneness and denies distinction. But seeing it even once, everything changes; it only takes one white crow.

God and I, we look different
God in long purple robes
With a halo and a throne and all
Me in Levis and t-shirt
No halo, no throne, no all
But when I drown in the Ocean
We're the same

25.

How do you get God to remove His costume so that you can see Him?

vesha- costume	haanataH removal of	svaatma- one's Self	darshanam realization

iisha- god	darshanaM realization	svaatma- one's Self	ruupataH essential nature

Removing your costume, you realize that your essential nature is the same as God's, and that neither of you exist, that you both are That ...

If you drop your costume, your attitude or belief in your reality as a separate entity, you will realize that you are That, essential nature. You will also see clearly that God is, in fact, also That, that all is One and that neither you, nor God, could possibly be different from That.

Costume, identity, story line gone
This emptiness, no one here, no one there
God also is out of luck
No me, no God
Only this dancing
Only One
All one
Alone
This

<u>26.</u>

How do you remain as this Self? How do you hold on to this realization?

aatma-	*saMsthitiH*	*svaatma-*	*darshanam*
self	effortless abiding	one's Self	realization

aatma-	*nirdvayaad-*	*aatma-*	*nishthataa*
self	non-dual	Self	abiding

Effortless abiding in the non-dual Self is realization.

Recognizing that your own true Self is the non-dual reality leads to a natural effortless abidance in the Self. This awareness or presence is your natural state and as it is always present. There is no need to worry about the possibility of losing it, even if thoughts or emotions do arise and appear to obscure it.

Abiding, effortless, Home at last
No one worried about doing it right or losing it
No way wrong, or right, no way at all
No one passing out grades on nothingness
No one deciding if reality is Real
Home, where it's always been
Home

27.

What else do you need to know if you obtain realization?

jnaana- knowledge	varjita- free from	ajnaanahiina- free from ignorance	cit consciousness
jnaanam- knowledge	asti kiM is there	jnaatum- to be known	antaram anything else

Abiding in Consciousness is beyond any knowledge or ignorance. If you abide There, there is nothing else to be known.

The realization that you are the Self, One, Consciousness, is beyond any traditional knowledge. Self is not accurately captured in anything that you have already learned, nor will you someday learn that critical piece of information that will clearly and completely be It. No objective knowledge will in any way add to what This is. There is no knowledge that you can acquire that will be the equal of this natural Peace, still and clear.

Thomas Aquinas, the famous Thirteenth Century Christian saint and one of the greatest theologians and philosophers of the Christian Church, when he was close to death and saw the Reality, said that all he had written was "like so much straw compared to what I have seen and what has been revealed to me". (15)

Knowing beyond a knowledge of things
No not knowing the right things
No knowing the wrong things
No hollowness craving more information
Not one more piece of information
Nothing to know or not know
Only This, only This

<u>28.</u>

<u>*What is your real nature?*</u>

kiM	*svaruupam-*	*ity-*	*aatma-*	*darshane*
what	my real natu	thus	the Self	recognition

avyaya-	*abhava-*	*apuurna-*	*cit-*	*sukham*
unchanging	unborn	always full	consciousness	happiness

Your real nature is unchanging, unborn, complete happiness.

If you inquire with deep curiosity into what your real nature it, you will see that it is the Awareness which sees the ever-changing body, thoughts and senses as objects. It is the unchanging screen upon which all of these appear. You realize that you are not those changing objects, but instead are that ever-present screen. You are that consciousness and complete happiness that never changes, that never begins or ends, and that requires nothing more to complete or fulfill it.

What am I really?
In the middle of the darkest night
Alone
What changes?
What doesn't?
Ever changing body, senses, thoughts or
Unchanging, uncreated, ever full, being, awareness
Which?

29.

Will you be liberated from being bound when you become Self aware?

bandha-	*mukty-*	*atiitaM*	*paraM*	*sukham*
bondage	liberation	beyond	limitless	happiness

vindatii-	*ha*	*jiiva-*	*stu*	*daivikaH*
attains	here	the individual	indeed	with divine virtues

Having the right predispositions, you will achieve that limitless happiness that is beyond the concepts of bondage and liberation.

This limitless, already present, uncaused, natural happiness is beyond all concepts of bondage and liberation. If you have the necessary clarity, insight and sincerity and a strong desire to know the Truth, you will arrive at this understanding.

Wanting beyond reason to know the Truth
Wanting it like my hair was on fire
Determined to be liberated whatever the cost
Willing to surrender everything
Even to surrender "me"
Then, seeing….
I was never bound
Nor needed to be liberated
Unending freedom, limitless happiness already here

<u>*30.*</u>

Are any other practices, efforts, rituals or renunciations necessary?

aham-	*apetakaM*		*nija-*	*vibhaanakam*	
I	destruction of		shining	the Self	

mahad-	*idaM*	*tapo*	*Ramana-*	*vaag-*	*iyam*
greatest	this is	sacrifice	Ramana	the teaching	this

Surrendering the "I" is the greatest spiritual practice and leads to Self Realization. This is Ramana's teaching.

Disassembling and surrendering your "I", or ego, leads you to realize and abide in the Self that you have always been. This surrendering of the "I" is the greatest renunciation, the greatest sacrifice, besides which all others tinkle like tiny bells. This is the teaching of Ramana Maharshi.

What do I need to give up?
The car, the money, the house, what????
No, not so easy
Give up the one doing the doing
Simpler, but much harder
The final great surrender
And the only one that matters
Only then, only then
That

B. *Nirvana Shatakam*—Six Verses on The State of Enlightenment, Freedom and Happiness by Shankara

Shankara's *Nirvana Shatakam*, composed over 1200 years ago, is an embodiment of the "not this, not this" (neti, neti) teaching of Advaita Vedanta that can lead to the state of enlightenment, freedom and happiness. I first learned this text from a fellow traveler one dark night on Maui many years ago. When we went to India to meet his teacher, one of the best known yoga teachers in the West today, it was clear it was a special text. Although it is not well known generally, and there is very little written about it, it is well known by many senior teachers and travelers.

Importantly, although there are many "not this, not this" lines, every verse of this six verse classic ends in an affirmation, a declaration of what you really are, which balances and responds to the negations. These verses are a personal declaration and celebration by Shankara of his own Self Realization. They are a powerful demonstration of the breadth and range of understanding encompassed of enlightenment. Many of the verses will seem evident and easy to grasp and accept. Others will challenge the very depths of your identity and understanding.

In this approach, every attachment, belief, experience, sensation, bodily segment or function is systematically considered and negated. Realizing that you cannot be both the subject and the object, each of these objectified elements is in turn rejected as being "not me". After negating everything that can be found to investigate, you are left with only the observer, and the investigation refocuses on the observer. When no observer is found, the entire dualistic structure collapses and everything is found to be That, One, or Beingness.

You can use the entire *Nirvana Shatakam* step by step, studying each line, each element, carefully, writing them down and pondering and investigating them. You can memorize and repeat them, or you can learn to chant them, which has been my approach for years. As you go through the process repeatedly, within each element, you will uncover, investigate, and discard layers and layers of identification, attachment and belief. Even after doing this process many times, you will be amazed at how subtle, and yet how deeply held your attachments and beliefs are, and how powerful the breaking of that identification is.

For each verse, the affirmation, the declaration, the refrain, is the same: "I am Awareness and uncaused happiness. I am everything. I am everything." Within this too, there is a question as to whether this is really your truth, or someone else's. Is this your reality? What does it mean to say that you are everything? Do the experiment and take the leap of faith that it might be true. Consider the possibility and what it would mean to you. What is your basic belief about your reality? Is there another possibility? Where did that belief come from?

The sequence of the verses is roughly in some order of degree of difficulty, for most folk. Some of the later ones, like those in the fifth verse, will challenge even the most experienced and dedicated practitioner. It is easier to assert with clarity and honesty, after some practice and inquiry, that on a real, and not just intellectual level, that you are "not these senses" in the first verse. However, in later verses, it will be much more challenging for most to have surrendered all attachments and identity with father, mother, partner, children, family, and friends, as well as pleasure, desire, security, and pride.

If you are repeating out loud or chanting, it is very effective to couple breath and meditating, or feeling, what each line means. With a long, slow and deep exhale, read or chant a single line out loud. On the subsequent inhale, mentally recite that line. Work your way through the entire teaching in a similar manner. After some time, try remaining mentally quiet during inhales and feeling the impact of the line, or just the silence that follows.

For lines with several items grouped within one word like "koshas", go mentally going through the individual items on the inhale, feeling them one-by-one and realizing that you are not that. During the reciting or chanting on the exhale, you can also feel the individual item with its Sanskrit word as you become more familiar with the text.

It is also helpful to focus on how each exhale and inhale is done. Not surprisingly, the most useful breathing sequence is that described under chanting, i.e. inhale "bottom up" and exhale "top down".

If you feel that you are unable to surrender some of your attachments, it is tempting to abandon this approach. This is usually accompanied by calling the approach unrealistic, world-denying, or nihilistic. You may then find another philosophy that will allow you to keep your remaining attachments under the guise of embracing the world. Your fear is what losing that attachment might mean to you, which is exactly the point of the work. This point is where great courage and intense desire to know the Truth are required. This is a swan dive into the unknown, trusting that all will be OK, that the teachings are true, and that your inmost request is not to be denied.

Some argue that it is important for them to embrace the world so that they can fix it. Ask yourself at this point whether the world told you that it needed repaired, or is that just your mind talking? Do you really believe that God was sitting on Her hands, powerless and clueless, just waiting for you, out of billions of folk on the planet over thousands of years, to come along and fix it? What is it that believes it is that important and powerful?

If you do surrender your attachments to, and identity with, those elements in *Nirvana Shatakam*, you will find what the phrase, "the peace that passeth all understanding" means. You will see for yourself what the statements "everything is One" and "you are That" really are saying.

Ramana Maharshi similarly gives this teaching in the answer to the question *Who Am I?* at the beginning of his classic of the same name as well as in the 22nd verse of *Upadesa Saram*:

You are not your body, senses, energies or mind; they have no voice, no beingness in themselves. You are the Beingness within which they occur.

There is also a very close parallel in the Heart Sutra, the Prajna Paramita Hrdaya Sutra, of the Buddhists. This is a staple in many Zen centers, including the local one at which I teach, and is often part of the daily morning service. Lines like "Form is exactly emptiness, emptiness exactly form" and "No eyes, no ears, no nose, no tongue, no body, no mind, no seeing, no hearing, … no thinking…" demonstrate the universality and power of this "not this, not this" teaching.

The verses are presented and numbered as they occur in the original work. There are at least two versions of *Nirvana Shatakam*. The main differences are in the first line of the fifth verse and parts of the sixth verse. The one used here is based on a version from an old scrap of tattered paper from a fellow traveler from his lineage and a more common version. The translation is a mix of several approaches including my own.

As this version is focused on smooth chanting, in several places "aH" has been replaced with "o" and "cit" is replaced with "cid." As Shiva is a complex concept for most Westerners, an alternative translation which goes to the essence of the concept is used. I added the summary and comments after each line to hopefully make the work more accessible.

1.

mano-	buddhy-	ahankaara-	cittaani	naaham
mind	intellect	I/ego	memory	I am not

I am not the mind that thinks or imagines, the intellect that categorizes and decides, the ego or "I" sense which springs into being as the "doer", nor the memory.

na ca	shrotra-	jihve	na ca	graanaa-	netre
nor	ear	tongue	nor	nose	eyes

I am not the ears that hear, the tongue that tastes, the nose that smells, the eyes that see, nor the sense of touch.

na ca	vyoma-	bhuume	na	tejo	na	vaayuH
nor	space	earth	nor	fire	nor	air

I am not composed of the classical elements of space, earth, fire, air or water.

cid-	aananda-	ruupaH	shivoham	shivoham
awareness	bliss	form	I am Shiva	I am Shiva

I am Awareness and uncaused happiness. I am everything. I am everything.

2.

na ca	prana-	sangyo	na	vai	panca-	vaayuH
not	prana	force	not	indeed	five	vital airs

I am neither the energy force (prana) that activates the body, nor the energies that it subdivides into (vayus or vital airs) that animate the vital functions of the body:

a) Prana—which energizes the respiratory system and upper chest

b) Apana—which energizes the excretory system and lower trunk and abdomen below the navel

c) Vyana—which energizes the circulatory system and all muscles, ligaments and tendons

d) Udana—which energizes the reactions of the body as well as swallowing, speaking and similar actions in the throat area and upper body

e) Samana—which energizes the digestive system and the region between the chest and the navel

I am also not the chakras, the different focal points that represent the energy present in different regions and functioning of the body and mind.

na	vaa	sapta-	dhatur	na	vaa	pancha-	koshaaH
not	indeed	seven	materials	not	or	five	sheaths/bodies

I am not composed of the seven materials out of which the body is constructed: skin, flesh, fat, blood, muscle, bone, and marrow. I am not the five sheaths/bodies/koshas:

a) Food sheath/body—Annamaya Kosha—physical, material body

b) Vital air sheath/body—Pranamaya Kosha—energies that maintain the physiological functions of the body and activate the body

c) Mental sheath/body—Manomaya kosha—memory, recognition, analysis, emotions, mind

d) Intellectual sheath/body—Vijnanamaya kosha-personality, conditioning, discrimination, decision-making

e) Bliss sheath/body—Anandamaya kosha—seat of: priya (desire), moda (achieving the object of desire), nanda (pleasure), pramoda (desire for repeat of that pleasure), and ananda (unending bliss beyond desire and cause)

The location of the sense of an I is often associated with a separate chakra called the hridaya located on the right side of the chest at the approximate height of the physical heart. This chakra is sometimes shown as associated with the Heart chakra (Anahata). It is discussed in Harish Johari's *Chakras* and in *The Serpent Power* by Sir John Woodroffe. Ramana sometimes located the I in the intellectual sheath (Vijnanamaya kosha.) Ultimately, as Ramana emphasized, you will find that this distinction falls away when the I is absorbed and you realize that everything is One.

na	*vaak-*	*paani-*	*paadam*	*na*	*copastha-*	*paayuu*
not	*speech organ*	*hands*	*feet*	*not*	*genitals*	*anus*

I am neither the organs of action (karmendriyah) nor any of their activities: larynx (speech), arms (grasping), legs (locomotion), sexual organs (sexual activity), anus and urethra (elimination).

cid-	*aananda-*	*ruupaH*	*shivoham*	*shivoham*
awareness	*bliss*	*form*	*I am Shiva*	*I am Shiva*

I am Awareness and uncaused happiness. I am everything. I am everything.

3.

na me	dvesha-	raagau	na me	lobha-	mohau
neither	disliking	liking	nor	greed	confusion/delusion

I am not my dislikes or likes for any person, place, thing, or experience. I am not the confusion, anger or greed that I have experienced.

mado	naiva me	naiva	maatsarya-	bhaavaH
vanity, pride	neither	nor	jealousy	state of being

I am not the pride in my possessions, achievements, skills, etc., nor am I the jealousy I feel for the possessions, achievements, skills, etc. of others.

na dharmo	na ca- artho	na kamo	na mokshaH
no duty	no security or wealth	no pleasure	no liberation

I am not the duties that have come to me to be done, nor the security that I imagine that I have obtained through relationships, possessions or achievements. I am not the pleasures that have been or will be enjoyed, nor any spiritual experiences or accomplishments that I have had or will have.

cid-	aananda-	ruupaH	shivoham	shivoham
awareness	bliss	form	I am Shiva	I am Shiva

I am Awareness and uncaused happiness. I am everything. I am everything.

4.

na	punyam	na	paapam	na	saukhyam	na	duhkham
no	virtue	no	vic	no	pleasure	no	pain

I am not my good deeds, nor my bad ones, nor have I accumulated any karma because of them. I am not the pleasures, nor the pains of my body, senses or mind.

na	mantro	na tertham	na vedaa	na yagnyaaH
nor	sacred chants	nor pilgrimages	nor scriptures	nor rituals

I am not the spiritual practices or activities that I have done, not the chanting of any sacred texts or mantras, not the travels or pilgrimages to spiritual places, nor the workshops, books or scriptures I have studied, nor any rituals that I have done.

aham	bhojanam	naiva	bhojyam	na	bhoktaa
I am	not act of enjoying	not	object enjoyed	nor	enjoyer

In any act that I appear to perform, experience or sense, I am not the object being experienced, the experiencing itself, or the experiencer.

cid-	aananda-	ruupaH	shivoham	shivoham
awareness	bliss	form	I am Shiva	I am Shiva

I am Awareness and uncaused happiness. I am everything. I am everything.

5.

na me	*mrtyu*	*shankaa*	*na me*	*jaati-*	*bhedaaH*
I have no	death	fear	nor any	birth/class	difference

I have no fear of death nor any distinction that has come to me because of the particular family, country, religion, financial situation, etc., into which I was born. I am unconcerned by death, unchanged by birth.

pitaa	*naiva*	*me*	*naiva*	*mataa*	*na*	*janma*
father	neither	have I	nor	mother	nor	birth

I do not have a father or mother, nor was I ever born.

na	*bandhur*	*na*	*mitram*	*guru-*	*naiva*	*shishyaH*
no	relations or family	no	friend	teacher	nor	disciple

I have no relatives, children, partner, family, friends, teachers or students.

cid-	*aananda-*	*ruupaH*	*shivoham*	*shivoham*
awareness	bliss	form	I am Shiva	I am Shiva

I am Awareness and uncaused happiness. I am everything. I am everything.

6.

aham	*nirvikalpo*	*niraa-*	*kaararupaH*
I am	without distinctions or dualities	free of	sense of form

I have no distinctions or qualities such as race, skin color, gender, age, education, nationality, etc. I have no form or shape.

vibhut-	*vyapya*	*sarvatra*	*sarv-*	*indriyaanam*
omnipresent	pervading	everywhere	all	senses

Being without distinctions or form, I pervade all the senses, existing everywhere, in everything, in every form. Penetrating everywhere, I am the soul/heart/inner reality of all the indriyas. (Indriyas include not just the traditional senses of seeing, hearing, tasting, smelling and touch, but also the organs of action, or karmendriyas, i.e. voice, arms, legs, genitals and excretory organs, and the four aspects of the antakarana/mind, i.e., ego, memory, mind and intellect.)

sada	*me*	*samaatvam*	*na*	*muktaH*	*na*	*bandhaH*
always	I am	equanimity (the same)	no	liberation	no	bondage

I am always the same, no matter the conditions, time, place, etc. As such, I am beyond any concept of being free or being bound.

cid-	*aananda-*	*ruupaH*	*shivoham*	*shivoham*
awareness	bliss	form	I am Shiva	I am Shiva

I am Awareness and uncaused happiness. I am everything. I am everything.

A recording of the chanting of *Upadesa Saram* and of *Nirvana Shatakam* is on the author's website at www.happiness-beyond-thought.com.

C. The *Bhagavad Gita*—Selected Verses

One of the classical works of world spiritual teaching, the *Bhagavad Gita*, which translates as the "Song of God" has been widely quoted and studied by Westerners as well including Thoreau and Emerson. Of the 700 verses in the most popular translations of this 2500 year-old work, many different selections have been made for study. Ramana Maharshi selected 42 verses as those most useful for awakening and presented them in *The Song Celestial*. From those 42, what follows are about a dozen that have been most useful in my practice and teaching. The order is different from what Ramana Maharshi suggested. The first verse is, however, the one verse that he thought was the most important one in the *Bhagavad Gita*. The verses are introduced by questions as in the earlier texts and are followed by what the verse means for me. Roman numerals indicate the Chapter which is followed by the verse.

There are many, many translations of the Gita to suit every taste and interest. They range from the exhaustive, clear and authoritative to the modern and poetic. Find one that suits your taste.

Giving this cornerstone of Hinduism as a key text does not imply that it has the unique insight into awakening among the world's great spiritual texts. Ramana himself, schooled in a Methodist Middle School and the American Mission High School, frequently quoted from the Christian Bible. One of his famous quotes is "the whole Vedanta (extensive portions of the Hindu Vedas focused on non-dual awakening) is contained in two Biblical Statements: 'I Am that I Am' and 'Be still and know that I am God.'"

What is the nature of the Self or Atman?

X, 20

aham-	aatmaa	gudaakesha	sarva-	bhuuta-	shaya-	sthitaH
I am	the Self	who is always awake	all	beings	heart	resides

aham-	adish-	ca	madhyaM	ca	bhuutaanaam-	anta	eva ca
I am	the creator	and	sustainer	and	all beings	dissolver	and

I am the Self, who is always awake, who resides in the hearts of all beings. I am the creator, maintainer and dissolver of all beings and things.

II, 20

na jaayate   mriyatae vaa kadaacin- na- ayaM bhuutva- abhavitaa vaa na bhuuyaH
is not born does not die or   ever   nor   this   having been cease to be or not again

ajo   nityaH   shashvato - ayaM puraano   na   hanyate hanyamaane sharere
unborn changeless eternal   that ever new is not destroyed is destroyed when body

This Self is not born and does not die. It is not that This, having been ever ceases to exist again. This Self is unborn, eternal, changeless and always new. It is not destroyed when the body is destroyed.

II, 24

acchedyo-   ayam   adaahyo- ayam   akledyo-   ashoshya   eva ca
cannot be cut This cannot be burned This cannot be wet cannot be dried also and

nityaH   sarva-gataH sthaanur-   acalo   -ayaM   sanaatanaH
changeless all pervading unmoving immovable   This   eternal

The Self cannot be cut, burned, wetted, or dried. It is changeless, all-pervading, motionless, immovable and eternal.

If you truly realize the Self, will you ever forget it or lose it?

XV, 6

na   tad-   bhaasayate   suuryo   na   shashaanko   na   paavakaH
not   That   illuminate   by sun   not   by moon   not   by fire

yad-   gatvaa   na nivartante   tad- dhaama paramam mama
there having gone   do not return   that abode   ultimate   is mine

Neither sun, moon nor fire illuminate That which is My ultimate abode. Those who reach there do not return.

If I surrender and become absorbed in the Self, will I be able to feed and care for myself and others?

IX, 22

ananyaash-		cintayanto	maam	ye janah	paryupaasate
not separate from		meditate on	me	those who	seek or recognize me

tesam	nitya-	abhiyuktanam	yoga-	kshemaM	vahamy-	aham
for those	always	awake to me	wants	losses they fear	take care of	I

I take care of the needs of those who seek Me, meditate on Me, see themselves as not separate from Me and see Me in everything.

What about surrender?

II, 71

vihaaya		kaamaan	yaH	sarvaan	pumaaM-	shcarati		niHsprhaH
having given up		desires	one who	all	person	moves around		without longing

nir-	mamao		nir - ahankaaraH		sa	shaantim-	adhigacchati
without the sense of mine			without the sense of "I"		he	peace	gains

The person who has given up all desires moves around without longing, without the sense of "I" or "mine", and gains peace.

How should you practice in order to know the Self?

VI, 25

shanaiH	shanai-	ruparamed-		buddhyaa		dhrti-	grhetayaa
gradually	gradually	may one resolve		with the intellect		endowed with discrimination	

aatma-	saMsthaM	manaH	krtvaa	na	kincid-	api	cintayet
in the Self	abide	mind	make	not	anything	else	think of

Gradually, gradually, with a discriminating intellect, make the mind abide in the Self and not think of anything else.

VI, 26

yato yato	nishcarati	manash-	cancalam-		asthiram	
for whatever reason	runs away	mind	restless		unsteady	

tatas- tato	niyamya-	itad-	aatmany	eva	vasham	nayet
for that reason	bring back	it	to the Self	alone	into your hands	bring it

For whatever reason, if the restless mind runs away, take it into your hands and bring it back to the Self alone.

If you become stabilized in the Self, is there anything else you need to do?

III, 17

ya- stv- aatma-	ratir- eva	syaad-	aatma-	trptash-	ca maanavaH
who in the Self	delights alone	would be	with Self	satisfied	and person

aatmany- eva	ca santushtaH	tasya	kaaryaM	na vidyate
in the Self alone	and contented	for him	work to be done	does not exist

One who delights in the Self, is satisfied with the Self and is content in the Self alone, has nothing else to do.

III, 18

naiva	tasya	krtena-	arthaH	na-	akrten -	eha	kashcana
not	for person	doing action	purpose	nor	not doing action	in this world	any

na ca-	asya	sarva- bhuuteshu	kashcid-	artha-	vyapaashrayaH
not and	for this person	all beings	any one	purpose	depending for any

For the Self-realized person, there is no purpose in doing or not doing something in this world. Nor does he depend on anyone else for achieving any purpose.

What will the state be when you are absorbed in the Self?

IV, 22

yadrcchaa-	laabda-	santushto	dvandva-	ateto	vi-	matsarah
by chance	what comes	content	opposites	unaffected by	without	jealousy

samaH	siddhaav-	asiddhau	ca	krtva-	api	na nibadhyate
the same	success	failure	and	performing action	even	is not bound

He is content with what comes by chance, is unaffected by pleasure and pain, and free of jealousy. He is the same in success and failure and is not bound even while performing actions.

Do actions stop when someone becomes absorbed in the Self?

XVIII, 61

iishvaraH	sarva-	bhuutaanaaM	hrddeshe	Arjuna	tishthati
god	all	beings	in the hearts	Arjuna	resides

bhraamayan	sarva-	bhuutaani	yantraa-	ruudhaani	maayayaa
to move	all	beings	machine	mounted	by magic

God resides in the hearts of all beings, Arjuna, and makes them all move by his magical power as if they were mounted on a machine.

How can you work with these teachings?

A powerful approach for working with these teachings is to treat them as chants and couple them with the breath and meditating on what each word or line means. After a long, slow and deep inhale, chant a single line of the teaching on the exhale. On the subsequent inhale, mentally recite that line of the chant. With the next exhale, chant the next line, and then subsequently recite that line mentally on the next inhale. Work your way through the entire teaching in a similar manner.

You may find that remaining quiet mentally on the inhales gives a deeper feeling of the line than does mentally repeating it. It may also be different for different lines. More complex lines with several grouped items will probably require mentally going through the items on the inhale, feeling them one-by-one.

Shorter, simpler lines can be felt syllable-by-syllable during the chanting on the exhale, particularly as the chants become more familiar.

As you work with the teachings, coordinating the breath with the chanting and abiding with that line, you will find that there are meanings on top of meanings, and, as different levels of that particular attachment or teaching are revealed, that insights change from day to day. This approach can be an invaluable window into understanding the structure of your own consciousness.

It is also helpful in working with these teachings, if your breathing is focused on how each exhale and inhale is done. Inhales are most effective if they are done from the "bottom up", i.e. first using the diaphragm, then the ribs/intercostals, then the shoulders/clavicle/upper chest. Exhales are most effective and supportive of the practice, if they are done "top down", i.e. upper chest, ribs, and then diaphragm. You will find that if you leave the contraction of the diaphragm to the end of the exhale, that this naturally creates stability and a gentle "lock" on your lower energy that supports the practice.

Chanting spiritual texts is a powerful practice and has a long tradition. The practice is called "parayana" and was strongly recommended by Ramana and many others. It can form a continuing core long after you believed you were beyond practice. Reportedly Nisargadatta chanted texts daily up until the very end of his life.

On a personal note, I had no interest in Sanskrit or in chanting for many years, despite having yoga teachers who were masters in it and who continually tried to interest me. However, when the page turned and the "I" blew out like a candle in the wind, amazingly, great interest arose for Sanskrit chanting, particularly for the three texts in this book. Nothing could have been more unexpected. It has continued for years. Just as it is, parayana arises daily or not, sometimes being 45 minutes to an hour, alternating with complete stillness. Other times it doesn't arise at all. The sequence of the chants varies. It arises in emptiness and goes on by itself with no apparent chanter doing it. How long it will continue and how it will manifest, I haven't a clue.

Questions and concerns raised in dialogue

It is often useful to see what questions others raise when engaged in the process. Many have the same questions but have either not formulated them completely or are afraid, for whatever reason, to ask the question themselves. What follows are some typical questions and answers that emerged in dialogue in small group discussions or from subsequent correspondence. There was no direct recording of the discussions because the recording process often changes the dynamic of the interchange, particularly in small intimate groups. With direct recording, there is often the concern about how this will sound to others, whether it will be wise or insightful enough, be foolish or be a good question, et cetera.

What was done in the place of direct recording is that soon after the dialogues, I wrote down what was remembered of the questions and answers. This approach, which is what was done in all recording of spiritual teachings before the advent of recording equipment, has some obvious limitations. Every attempt has been made to make it as true to the intent and content of the discussion as possible. I subsequently checked these entries with the questioners to verify the record of the discussion. Several of these are from direct correspondence and are exactly as they occurred except for changing the names.

It is important in reading such discussions to remember that each answer arises in emptiness as it arises and is appropriate for that questioner at that time. The answer is to further the awakening process, not to make someone feel good, be consistent or put forth some preset doctrine that everyone will like. The answer may well not be your answer. In larger groups, it is likely that someone will disagree with the answer given to another. However, it is exactly those answers that in my experience are most effective at working directly with the actual questioner. Sometimes the results of the answer don't arise until some time later.

If you read or attend such discussions, be aware of consistency. If you see total and complete consistency with a variety of questioners and questions, it is unlikely to be coming from clarity and emptiness; it is likely coming from a carefully learned repertoire of answers designed by someone's mind. It is unlikely to be appropriate to the actual question or questioner.

Q. If I become enlightened, isn't there a possibility that without an "I" that I will become a menace to society, being irresponsible, and hurting and abusing others?

A. If you become enlightened, what will happen is that you will see others, and everything, at its basic level as the same ONE, the same thing, and in some strange way, inside of, or contained within an awareness that doesn't really have a doer. What occurs is that you will be helping yourself, as it is appropriate and as it arises. Why would you not help yourself? With the loss of the I identity and its conditioning, your actions will arise out of nothingness and will be completely appropriate to the situation at hand. Your actions will not be encumbered by some hoped for recognition, reward in heaven, or some previous model of what you should do that you have been conditioned to believe is right. Without an I, there will also be no residue of the action, no clinging to the result or judging its merit or outcome. It will be done, completely finished. Then something else will arise, as it arises.

Q. If I become enlightened, I am afraid that I won't be able to function in the world and earn a living and will become poor and homeless and that my children will suffer. How do I know that I will be OK?

A. I continued to work very successfully for years in complex industrial and institutional management roles requiring much apparent responsibility, knowledge, action and decision making. I also had a family, children, possessions, et cetera, and had an intensive spiritual practice, both before and after the big shift occurred. Loss of functioning just isn't what happens.

As Ramana Maharshi said; "The feeling 'I work' is the hindrance. Inquire, 'Who works?' ... It will go on automatically. Make no effort either to work or to renounce work....If you are not destined to work, work cannot be had even if you hunt for it. If you are destined to work, you will be forced to engage in it." (16)

Decisions, knowledge and actions arise, as they are required, perfectly appropriate to the situation without the functioning of thought or the need for an I. The actions are normally of higher quality and clarity than was previously the case because they are not clouded by the on-going chatter, confusion and second-guessing of the mind/I. You are fully present for the discussion and decision, rather than being off someplace else in your mind. Others are rarely even aware of any big change occurring. Many Self-realized folk change little or nothing about their external lives.

One of the most revealing and useful things is actually meeting and talking with reputedly enlightened folk, and seeing what they look like and how they behave. It is not like what we are conditioned to believe they should look like or how they should behave. The annual Inner Directions Gatherings at La Jolla, that are unfortunately now discontinued, provided a wonderful opportunity to see, hear, and talk in a gathering, and possibly 1/1, with some prominent enlightened folk. These folk were from many spiritual traditions: Jewish rabbis, Hindus, Buddhists, Zen monks, Christian monastics, Sufis, African tribal leaders, et cetera. None of them would stand out in a shopping mall or on a city street, except for the few who wore some different traditional dress.

This may be bad news if you had planned on having a beautiful robe, a special soft, deliberate, slow way of speaking, long flowing hair, and moving in a slow, god-like way, but that is what happens.

Q. Do you ever get pulled out of the silence or presence?

A. Even after the page has turned, there will still be thoughts occasionally arising. Normally the thoughts will pass across consciousness like birds in an empty sky with little attention paid to them. However, there will be times when a deeply held attachment or relationship may still have a hook, either sharp or dull, that can pull one into the world. The most useful approach is to welcome this as something to be worked with, inquire to whom it comes, and then watch it subside. Even if there is a thought loop that recurs, it will be intermittent and surrounded by awareness and consciousness. Eventually it too will die away.

Tony Parsons, in talking about this, said that his life moved back and forth between "me-ing" and being, or between the world and being. The books and videos are full of instances where reputedly enlightened folk manifested what appeared to be very real emotions and attachments. Buddha is said to have cried when he learned of a war starting in an adjacent land in which his relatives lived. Christ threw the money changers out of the temple. Ramana Maharshi would get upset with questioners. Nisargadatta Maharaj, as you can see in his videos, had a fiery personality and frequently threw people out of his room if he believed they were not serious. The most important thing is to not redevelop a me that acts as the police of whether this enlightenment is good enough and whether or not I am showing too much emotion, etc. What emerges will be what emerges. Welcome it, and if it persists, inquire into who has this thought, et cetera.

There are some important physiological things to remember that will make the emergence of, or persistence of, residual thoughts less likely. Ramana stressed the importance of sattvic food, or food that neither stimulates nor induces tiredness and dullness. There is much written in the yoga texts on sattvic food, and bookstores are full of food books. The most useful advice that I received on food and meditation was from one of my first yoga teachers who told us to keep a food diary and record the effects of different foods on our mental state. There is no greater source of information that what really does happen to you; it may be different than what is written in the books and it may change from time to time.

Another critical aspect is the need for sufficient energy. In my experience, if the body/mind is tired, there is a much higher likelihood of thoughts emerging. In fact, for me, the best indicator of when the body/mind is tired is when thoughts begin to arise. J. Krishnamurti has discussed this extensively in his teachings.

Q. When I come here and sit with you, it is so easy to get into a deep quiet, space. But when I go to a sesshin (intensive Zen meditation session), however, it is so excruciatingly painful. Does sesshin serve any purpose?

A. There is a place early in your practice when it is important to develop enough ability to concentrate so that you can be a witness, to be able to be present to observe thoughts, so that serious inquiry can be done. Many techniques from hatha yoga and tai chi to breathing exercises and subject/object dualistic meditation such as practiced often in Zen can be useful in this regard. The challenge is to not get stuck there. Techniques will not take you to non-dualistic awakening as there will always be an I doing the practice. The more advanced your practice becomes in your mind, the more the ego can grow.

As to the levels of pain and suffering that can develop in some practices, like Zen, it can be useful to develop some detachment so that you can recognize the difference between pain and suffering. There can be pain in the body, but suffering is a mental phenomenon that happens to a "me". There is no value to some of the masochistic extents to which these practices can go. If you go to India you can see sadhus holding one of their arms over their heads for years, or standing on one leg for a decade, or practicing self-mutilation. It is extremely difficult to do such a practice without developing an enormous ego, which is the problem you were trying to solve in the first place. As the Buddha found, this path just doesn't work; too bad the sadhus didn't read that or didn't believe him.

If you don't know where you are in this pain/gain continuum, and whether it is of any value, ask "Who is doing the practice?" If there is someone there doing the practice, attached to its result and growing more austere by the day, you are on the wrong railroad.

Finally, there is nothing in any of these practices that requires that you hurt yourself in any way. Be fully mindful of what your body is saying; if there is real, acute pain, stop. At some level you will suffer until you stop. It is better to stop sooner rather than later. There are many practitioners with the scars to prove it.

Q. When I listen to you speak, you seem to be speaking from a state that is different from traditional dualistic practices. How do I get there with these practices?

A. With physical postures, breathing exercises and meditation, it is possible for most people to reach a state of stillness with few thoughts, if only for a short time. This stillness, although sweet and seductive, is not the end point. If you watch carefully, that stillness can also be produced by satisfying desires, removing unpleasant sensations or situations, or by a peak experience in any activity, whether it is hang gliding, playing chess, rock climbing, dancing, running, painting, sculpting, or whatever your passion, as Mihaly Csikszentmihalyi described in his classic book *Flow*.

Unfortunately, as everyone has observed, that temporary stillness is followed by a relentless return of thoughts. Awakening is different, however, in that the stillness becomes the ever present ground. Thoughts may still occur, but more like a few birds moving easily across the summer sky rather than the typical mental state which is like being in the middle of a huge flock in a migration. The big difference is that the Velcro is gone from the thoughts. You don't normally get caught by them.

Ramana Maharshi pointed out the difference between these two mental states in *Upadesa Saram*, when he described these two states as "manolaya", or temporary stilling of the mind and "manonasa", or absorption or elimination of the mind. "Laya vinashane ubhaya rodhane, laya gatam punar bhavati no mrtam." Laya is only temporary and the mind is reborn, but in manonasa, it is not.

Ramana went on to describe what to do when one has reached that temporary stilling of the mind. "Prana bandhanal lina manasam, Eka cintanah nasam ety adah." When your mind is stilled through control of the breath, meditate on the One to absorb the mind. The important step is to not be content to rest in that stillness or peace, but to go further, and use the inquiries, "What hears?", "Who am I?" and "Where am I?" If you use this stillness to open the door to deepening inquiry, rather than just a place to hang out, there is the opportunity to absorb what we call the mind and the I and change the nature and operation of thought.

Q. Do I need to withdraw from the world and create a perfect environment that completely supports my meditation to become enlightened? It seems to me that running away from relationships, with the things that push my buttons, is avoiding the real work that needs to be done.

A. As one of my early teachers said, "You do not need to create problems to work on; the world is perfectly capable of providing them all by itself". That has certainly been my experience.

As to perfect environments, if you are identified with your body/mind, there are no perfect environments. You can go to the most remote and sacred cave, jungle or mountain but "no matter where you go, there you are". If you are not identified with your body/mind, it doesn't matter where you are. In actuality, although you like to believe that you are in charge of this decision, you will be placed in the right environment whether you want it or not. Everything that happens to you will be, as Ram Das has said, "grist for the mill of enlightenment". Everything always is perfect, just as it is, including your environment.

Q. Will I develop special powers if I do this practice? What might they be? Will it be like Kundalini experiences?

A. Kundalini experiences are just experiences and energy moving through the body, perhaps releasing some long held blocks. The important thing is to not become attached to them. An enormous drama can develop around who has which experience, how intense it is, what it means, et cetera. Forget about it. What happens will happen. Let go of it and it will ultimately pass.

As far as special powers or siddhis, they may or may not develop, and that will be just as it is. In my case, they developed unexpectedly. They were in the areas where I had the greatest attachments; I could get what I wanted most. The ego and the attachment to the want grew enormously, in exactly the wrong direction if one wants to awaken. They are hindrances. If they develop, just let go of them, although I realize from first hand experience that is easier said than done. When you realize for yourself that they are a great barrier to opening, you will drop them.

Q. Knowing you makes all the difference. It makes it seem possible. You have talked about everything being unreal, a dream, all being One. Although the descriptions from Self-realized people are quite similar in this regard, for some, life seems to become completely meaningless. Nisargadatta said "For you this life is everything. To me it is nothing". For others this life remains a portal, a way to witness the manifested and to have great joy in the unfolding of the manifested. Could you talk about that?

A. When Nisargadatta says "To me it is nothing", he is saying that this life, the world, et cetera, have no fundamental importance or significance to him as they are, in Truth, unreal. Nisargadatta and Ramana still functioned very effectively in the world. They responded when their name was called, they had no problem finding where lunch was, answering complex questions, et cetera. There was a residual functional I there to the end.

At the same time, it was clear to them that the world is unreal. One metaphor is of a mirage: we know it is unreal, that it isn't really water and we can't drink it, yet still we see it and can even marvel at it.

Another analogy is that of a movie, or a play. We watch the movie or the play, perhaps become deeply involved and forget ourselves, and yet, with just a slight look away, we know it is unreal and we are out of it.

Another metaphor is that of a dream, completely mentally constructed and unreal, yet while you are in the dream all dream objects, folks and happenings seem totally real.

Seeing directly that the world is a dream is one of the strangest and most unexpected things. Although I had read a little about this before the shift occurred, it had no meaning. I was totally unprepared for what actually unfolded.

As long as there are attachments, and you live from the viewpoint of identity with the body, or with the mind, you will not see that the world is a dream. If you do see the unreality, everything changes, everything.

Q. Possibly the most significant practice that I have learned here is about acceptance. Loving what is. As Eckhart Tolle says, "Treat everything that happens in your life as if you chose it". Maybe at the outset of this practice I had some realization that I didn't know what was best for me, that I created my own unhappiness. I have been somewhat successful in giving up the illusion of control. Even when bad things happen … I try to offer no resistance. I watch for any negativity or urge to complain and examine it. And the feedback has been good. The more I let go the happier I seem to be.

A. We are not in control of our lives. That's not just a supposition. Take any incident in your life and try to trace back all of the factors that would have to have occurred to bring it into manifestation. How many of them did you have any kind of conscious control over? As you do something, try to imagine what effect it will have on everyone it touches in the future. Do you have any such knowledge or control? If you had no control over how it got here and don't know what is going to happen when you do something, how can you not accept this as perfect just as it is?

Q. This girl has kind of made her way into my life and we had ended up having sex. During sex, I took this sort of leap of faith and it just didn't seem real. Afterwards, there were a lot of complications with her current boyfriend and they broke up and I feel guilty. What should I do?

A. Having sex and not being attached to it, and having it not seem real, like it wasn't happening to you, is what can occur if you are fully present. It is strange when it occurs, but it is possible for there to be sublime and ecstatic sensations and yet not be there as someone experiencing them.... The less of you there is during the experience, the less attachment there will be to the experience afterwards.

Having your mind come in afterwards and create all sorts of guilt, placing you in charge of a broken relationship, or being responsible for whatever she might do with that experience, is just another trick of the mind and is foolish.

You are not responsible, because you can't really control, and can't predict or know, all of the results of your actions and what impact they might have. You don't know what the right outcome should be ...

The important learning is that you focus...on what is going on with you. What was your awareness? What did you feel afterwards? Did the mind come in and quickly make it an experience and begin causing difficulties and conflicts?

Watch for your attachment and aversions. See if you can be fully present for what occurs. Don't blame her for the relationship; she is also part of the divine dance and is dancing as she is supposed to. Honor and respect that. Remember that she is also part of the One, part of you. Whatever happens, happens and is perfect just as it is.

As the *Ribhu Gita* says "Those engaged in the pursuit of knowledge of the Brahman-Self, happening to get involved in the mundane pleasures of sex, should regard such pleasures as merely faint shadows of the bliss of the Self."

Sex can be found to be just that. Even at its most ecstatic and sublime, a faint shadow of the bliss of the Self. That doesn't mean you forcefully engage in a celibate life prematurely. As you progress, you may find that the bliss of the Self really transcends all and that sex, like all pleasures, drops away like autumn leaves fall from a tree.

Q. *I am currently getting to know some spiritual women and determining if there is a romantic connection between us. Some women want children. Some women don't and just want to dive deep spiritually. Is there any ancient or modern spiritual wisdom about whether or not to have children? Do you have any advice? I feel like I should make this decision up front about whether I want a family or not. But if I go with the flow and be in the moment, it seems wrong to make up my mind ahead of time.*

A. The ancient approach was for someone certain of pursuing a spiritual path to take sannyas, or renounce completely, everything, including home, marriage, children, possessions, et cetera. This could take place either early or later in life after they had completed the four classical stages of student, householder, retired person and sannyasi or renunciate. Not everyone went through them all in order as some took sannyas directly, but the typical path led through a traditional evolution ending in renunciation.

Ramana Maharshi did not advocate sannyas (renunciation), saying repeatedly that sannyas was not the physical renunciation, but the renunciation of one's ego. An often quoted line was "The man who is active in the world and yet remains desireless, without losing sight of his essential nature, is alone a true man." Also, "… better than the man who thinks 'I have renounced everything' is the one who does his duty but does not think.… 'I am the doer' … a householder who does not think 'I am a householder' is truly a sannyasi."(17)

Many, many folk asked Ramana if they could take sannyas, but he uniformly dissuaded them even though he was probably the truest example of a classical sannyasi in modern times meditating in caves in silence for over a decade starting at the age of 16.

I have two daughters and they, along with my wife, have been great teachers. Few things can so expose your remaining attachments and areas for further work than your children or your marriage.

Finally, however, whatever you decide will be the right decision as it can't come out any other way. Your decisions are only apparent.

Q. *I've been thinking about what I miss the most since I've been unable to come to our weekly gatherings. It is this particular space. I don't recall accessing it elsewhere, even in deep retreats. My empirical side is active these days, so I think I see a trend here. Now that I think about it, I felt it at Sriramanasramam (Ramana Maharshi's Ashram) in Tiruvannamalai.*

I asked you about 3 months or so after we met whether you employed some sort of shakti (energy) in the room when we sit. We talked about the dangers of the siddhis (powers) and the traps of shakti. I'm just wondering why I can't replicate the results elsewhere.

A. On whether or not I employ some shakti, there really isn't any I here, so there is no creator of shakti. Shakti just is. I have no idea where it, or anything else for that matter, comes from.

What you have felt when we were together is highly dependent on one's spiritual maturity and openness. Some felt Ramana's great transformative energy, others felt nothing....

As Ramana frequently said, the great teaching happens in silence. We talk in weekly meetings to entertain the mind while the real work goes on underneath constantly when we are together.

As far as siddhis and shakti traps, it's not clear to me how siddhis manifest, only that they do. Interestingly, siddhis manifested for me where I had the strongest desires. The temptation to misuse the siddhis is great until you see that using them to attempt to satisfy your desires only leads into more desire, bondage and dissatisfaction. If you don't see this and don't step away, you will become caught.

Q. I found your statement: "Sincerity and diligence are the keys. Question everything" very powerful. I am doing my best to make my entire life, including my business life, united and simplified towards the one goal of awakening. In dating, getting to know women that might be potential matches for me, I am sincere and authentic about my spiritual life and try to reflect my spiritual beliefs in every sentence that I communicate to them or anyone else in my life.

A. With regard to business life, in my experience, functioning in the work world goes on with enhanced clarity and creativity as one reduces the chatter of the self-referential mind. Every interaction can be met without a prior agenda or personal history, and with detachment, so the situation can be seen clearly just as it is at that moment and performance can be what will appear as extraordinary.

At the same time, I found that because there was less personal fear and insecurity you may not be willing to play the politics that are advantageous in the corporate world. Even if you are performing at a superior level, you may find yourself operating at a disadvantage in reaching the highly political upper levels.

Remember, again, that none of this is ultimately within your control, only apparently so. It will be as it is. Just drop your expectations of how it is supposed to be.

I did not find any value in proselytizing my understanding or path at work. Very few are ready to listen. For most folk, work is about work. Do what comes to you to be done from a space of clarity and detachment, and work will take care of itself. What is supposed to happen will happen, no matter what you want.

In selecting a potential partner, my experience is that you need to be open about your efforts on the path, but recognize that your partner may not share those feelings, nor does she need to also be on the path. It is important that she needs to be open to allowing you the space to be as you are. This is a threat to most partners as it can place them in a position of being #2, which may be unacceptable.

Also recognize that both of you will change significantly, likely in dissimilar ways. Many senior spiritual teachers have experienced considerable relationship difficulties of all sorts as they underwent significant changes.

Q. In my meditation I was doing self-inquiry on sounds, for example "from where is this heater hiss bubbling up out of" ... sink into that ... "what is it that creates this ticking clock?" ... sink into it. And each time, just as the thoughts that I had questioned subsided, these physical sounds subsided too as I sank into the Self. The senses were there but they were unimportant, almost as though I wasn't in need of them because there was a light shining out from me; I didn't even care about my senses because the warmth of the light was strong and unquestioning and all right with everything because it was the light that mattered only ... Is this real? Is this truly what it's like?

A. Yeah, that'll do.... Realize that life goes on, as it goes on, even as you are abiding in the Self. Self-realization is all about abiding in, or being, that Presence, Stillness, Silence, even if you get drawn out of it from time to time by activities or the mind. It is there all the time. It is not something to be gotten. It is already and always there, and is seen if the rest of the mental junk gets out of the way.

Be careful not to make these into experiences. Recognize that they will come and go as they come and go and are of no real importance. Use them as you have, with inquiry into "Who is hearing this sound?", "Where does this I, thought or recognition of this experience, come from?" or "Who is observing this experience?"

Many folk become experience junkies and collect, compare and parade these experiences around, but in the end this becomes an impediment that can really strengthen the ego and the hold of the mind.

Q. Which came first, the chicken or the egg?

A. The chicken.

Q. I have found working with the affirmation you gave me to be very effective. I stopped doing it for a week because life was flowing so well I thought I didn't need it, but old anxieties returned, so I'm doing it again.

In my Zen sitting meditation sessions I have been using breath counting, but have always had big reservations about it. I used to think it was silly to count when one is trying to think about nothing. Also, I do not know how to go about inquiry while on the cushion unless I am listening to you. What practice should I do?

A. On sitting, it isn't useful to accept and reject meditation approaches quickly. The mind typically is fascinated with a new technique for a short while and then wants to move on to another approach. That is how the mind avoids any serious investigation, by never agreeing to participate in any serious inquiry. The mind decides that this approach is trivial, that one is obtuse and unsuited for Westerners, another is intended only for advanced folk, another only for raw beginners and simple folk, this one isn't working fast enough, et cetera.

As you have had good success with the affirmation, I would recommend that you spend six weeks using it as your meditation on your cushion as well as using it throughout the day. As you have seen, abandoning it doesn't work.

Meditation is really preparing us for everyday life, so the two should not be different. Don't just blindly parrot the affirmation during your meditation, but while you are sitting, inquire into it to see if it is true or not. Try it seriously, watch the mind's resistance to the process, and just keep coming back to it. Give it a strong effort for six weeks; I think you will be surprised at the progress and impact. Check back with me with how it's going.

With regard to breath counting, the reason that breath counting is so often initially given is that it is an effective device to teach concentration to beginners and although it appears incredibly simple, very few can do it. The mind consequently rejects the approach as it doesn't want to be shown to be out of control; so out of control that it can't even allow counting to ten without disrupting the process. Breath counting is so powerful that at one sesshin the roshi had everyone, experienced and beginner, do nothing but breath counting.

However, as you have strong resistance to it and the affirmation, which is normally a later practice, has been working, I would continue with the affirmation. Others may be advising you to take the traditional sequential route starting with breath counting, but if it's not your practice, it's not your practice. Trust your own deepest intuition on the choice, which is not to be confused with the monkey mind; it will not fail you.

Q. At last night's gathering, when you were answering my question, although I was interested in what you were saying, I was distracted by the parakeet and missed what you said. I apologize for simply not giving you full attention. I would email the parakeet to apologize to him also, if I knew his email address.

A. It was really terribly unfortunate that you were distracted by the parakeet at just that instant. It had occurred, as a blinding flash, that "the essence of all of the teaching of non-duality can be summarized as ..." when you were distracted. After I said it, it was immediately snatched from consciousness and lost forever. Well, maybe next life.

The parakeet was supposed to make that noise at just that time, and the message may have been just that, about being attentive. It was apparent to you, to the parakeet and to me because you are so attentive and such a careful listener, that it was unusual for you to be distracted, but that was just as it was.

The parakeet and I have had a good laugh/chirp about it; we had planned it all carefully in advance as a Zen trick on you, and we caught you.

Q. I am not the doer. Self is not the doer. The gunas are the doer. Or as you have said "things just happen". Or as Suzuki Roshi has said: "Things as It is." Is this a correct understanding? Or is my need to credit "someone" with responsibility simply more ignorance?

If this is a correct understanding, then is it also correct that the gunas "make effort"? If so are gunas making the effort to remove the ignorant notion: " 'i' am not yet Realized"? Does my buddy, "Gunas" get all the credit?

Is this logical, that "i" am not making this effort? Is it appropriate to simply let the effort, or lack of it (as might be-or appear to be-the case), happen as it does and not be concerned with the "fruits" as Krishna instructs Arjuna?

A. Not only are you not the doer, but you are NOT. Your buddy Gunas is doing the dance without you, whether or not you give him credit, whether or not you believe you make effort or not. The gunas could care less about you, in all reality, as you are just a phantom to them. They are just dancing, dancing, dancing.

If it is helpful, the dance of the gunas can be looked upon as being done so that you can realize that you are not and that there is no you to realize anything.

Whether or not the apparent, fictional you decides to simply let the action take place by itself or not is of no real consequence; action is taking place by itself. Action doesn't need your permission or apparent participation to continue. There is ultimately no you to be concerned about any fruits or not. You are a construct of mind.

The good news is that you and everything else is the ocean, not just the waves. Creating an imaginary entity to worry about a particular wave is meaningless. It's all just ocean.

Q. I recently noted in my practice that the space at the end of the breath has gotten longer just as you said it would some time ago. This space is interesting. In meditation I look for it. I would not say that it is an infinite sea of calm. In fact it is sometimes accompanied by a shortness of breath and seems to require effort to stay with it, to extend it, to keep thoughts at bay. But in some way it feels like I am that, like it is just being. I am curious why it is elusive, why I can't seem to just be in that space.

It brings up the question I've often asked. How does one be earnest in their seeking, desire awakening above all else, pursue it like one's hair was on fire, AND just be still-ness, effortless being with nothing to attain, just be?

A. The space at the end of the breath is a window in or through for the imaginary I to realize that it is only an overlay on the unchanging Reality.

The shortness of breath, the feeling that it will slip away, the efforts to extend it, are just thoughts trying to hold on to yet another experience, to make it a possession, something that thought does as an I, a job that "I" am performing for "you," when in fact both are fictitious.

You are just that stillness, and only That, as you acknowledge that you feel in some way. You feel it because it is true.

The reason that you can't be in that space is that you are what is keeping that space from being. The existence of an I trying to be in that space, makes it impossible for it to be seen. The conundrum is that the I insists on having the experience of its not being there. It's not possible.

There is no one, really, no one, to be earnest, to practice, to have one's hair on fire. When that is realized, that effortless, natural, omnipresent space will be there, just as it always has been, and you will be identified with, absorbed in and lost in that omnipresence.

Q. Can you recommend a practice for me?

A. Be still.

Q. Your answer to the question of the doer struck a note; "Self realization is really realizing that you are just awareness, just that". In that moment it seemed simple and clear. Since then I'm watching closely how little my thoughts are connected to the body's actions. It's really quite amusing. As you say, there is awareness, little split seconds, yes, the traffic light is red, but most the time it's out there spinning away.

The thoughts in my head most the time now are "I am not this body, I am not these thoughts, but if not who am I?" … I keep wondering what the correlation is, if any, between the awareness that you are and this body. You certainly don't get to witness the illusion through any other body.

A. Your body is the apparent sensory, actioning pod surrounding your awareness, not some other pod, to be sure. The realization is not that there aren't sensory inputs through this apparent assemblage, but that the assemblage does not form who you are, is not what you are. Sound is categorized, analyzed and made into a problem through the action of the mind. What YOU are is not the mind, senses or the body. It is the awareness within which those manifest.

The work is to recognize those associations, those habitual fusions that have taken place between the mind, the senses and body to create an imaginary entity that believes it does these actions and takes on a reality of its own. Once you see these fusions, these associations, and realize that there is an awareness separate from them, the movement occurs from the belief that one is that imaginary entity into a recognition that one is that awareness.

Can you not be that awareness? Is it possible to believe that the awareness exists apart from you? Is awareness somewhere else and created by our actions? If body, mind, and senses are fleeting, "you" need to be somewhere. Where would you be— in awareness or in the changing scenario? You must continually exist someplace, or else you would be in continual amnesia having to recreate yourself every second. Are you the changing body, mind and senses, or are you the ever present awareness?

If you really were the changing body, mind and senses, where would you plant your existence?

As we discussed, Self realization is realizing that you are just awareness, just That. When you do, the attachments to the dance of the body/mind/senses falls away and with it the tyranny of thought.

Q. What does a realized person act or look like? I have heard that the Buddha's enlightenment was so extraordinary that people flocked to follow him.

A. In my experience, there is no apparent external manifestation that accompanies enlightenment that is discernable and consistent. There is no distinguishable careful and slow speech pattern. There can often be what looks like emotion. There are no special clothes, no special movements in a slow and thoughtful way, and no special aura. In fact, the belief that there is some special behavior or clothes has led to a great deal of manipulation of the true believers by those who pretend to be enlightened.

I have had the opportunity to see many reputedly enlightened folk, some of whom I studied closely with. We also have detailed recordings in many types of media of enlightened folk who are no longer in form, like Ramana Maharshi, Nisargadatta Maharaj, J. Krishnamurti, Poonjaji, etc. One could hardly imagine a broader spectrum of behaviors and personal attributes.

The only distinguishing characteristic that I have ascertained, and one often cited, is what happens to you when you are around enlightened folk over a period of time, and that experience is not universal. Some felt Ramana Maharshi's transformative energy, for example, while others felt nothing.

The big disadvantage that we have when we talk about Buddha, Jesus, Moses, Dogen, et cetera, is that we have no direct records except for the remembrances of devotees. Additionally, in the time frame in which many of the leaders of today's religions lived, the traditions were largely oral with a high percentage of illiteracy. Reportedly, no one wrote down anything about the Buddha until many years after he had died, so reports about what he was like, or what he did, are uncertain.

Q. After meeting two weeks ago... ... a veil was lifted, of course unexpectedly. All of a sudden there was recognition that I'm not my thoughts. Everyone always says it but I never felt it. It turns out I'm actually not the voice in my head that says stuff. That's separate from me. Immediately after was the recognition "I am awareness", though, of course, I don't think those words manifested until afterwards, when Steve (not his real name) came to claim the memory. The veil immediately dropped...So you're right about that. Steve really is ad-hoc. Thoughts occur, feelings occur, body occurs ..., I witness. They're separate pieces, and I don't think they need to be strung together ... It's so big, though, the feel. I am AWARENESS, not just "Steve is aware"....Better: awareness is aware. I think it's less personal than "Steve" ... It's crazy. I never looked at the looker before ... Steve's like 25 years old; all that witnessing and no question of the subject.

It's so weird that a recognition of this is born and dies. How can awareness once again identify itself with the voice in Steve's head? ... The "identification room" isn't big enough for the two of them, though ... Steve's still laboring under the impression that he's gonna get something in the end ... regardless of what I want, what is is and what will happen will happen.

A. Perfect, just as it is. Although all of that stuff that you have been hearing is true, it is, however, of no importance. The only thing that matters is that you have verified directly, first-hand, that it is true and not just some metaphysical Eastern b.s. You really are that permanent deathless Awareness.

Awareness hasn't reidentified with the voice in Steve's head. Even when the voice is going full tilt, see what is watching the stream of thoughts. It's awareness, always there, unchanging. The I, thoughts, desire, sensations, etc. may return with full force, but there is always awareness watching its return, departure, return, etc. Which of these is more real, more present, more True, the "I" or awareness?

The I rushes back in to try to reclaim "its" territory and will spend a great deal of time trying to explain, modify, recreate, take credit for, etc. that glimpse. Still, still, there is the deep knowing that what IS is beyond the I, beyond the mind, beyond thoughts, body, emotions, etc. and is always there, always. And it is, as you say, what you really are.

As you are present with, do not buy into the trick the I creates of generating a doer who is going to do something to get back to "beyond the I", "beyond the mind", an impossibility. How can the I, which is a thought, using the mind, get beyond thought, to the indescribable? ... .

Be watchful and aware of the dance of your thoughts and see that awareness is there always and you are that. You have become wise to the point of knowing that it is all out of your hands, always has been, always will be. Whatever unfolds is just as it should be, always perfect.

You cannot be other than awareness, no matter how hard you try.

Biography

Biographies and personal histories are of intense interest to others. It is not clear whether knowing this information is of any real value or if it just adds more confusion, but it arises so often that it is easier to include one. It is important to remember that a biography is only one version of the story, always remembered incorrectly and from a highly subjective standpoint. Recent brain studies have shown that the brain does modify long-term memories, perhaps because it too gets bored with them.

Unless you've read ahead, you know by now that all of these experiences happened to no one, and they ultimately mean nothing. The events and situations were created out of the control of an "I" and arose from nothingness and went into nothingness. An "I" was used as the subject here, rather than the standard third person approach like your mother wrote it, but both are equally incorrect. Attaching any importance, ownership, or personal causation to these chance remembrances is foolish.

As one of my Zen teachers, Toni Packer, said frequently, "Whatever happens to you is none of your business". Or, as Rumi has said, "Your life is not your own".

I was raised in a devout Methodist home and through early adolescence was involved in religious activities and even gave some religious talks. From early adolescence until late twenties, I lived a secular life with marriage, two children, undergraduate school, nuclear submarine service, and then graduate school. I did, however, at some deep level even as a kid, know that despite much conventional Christian teaching to the contrary, that it was possible for everyone to experience the consciousness of which Jesus spoke. I don't know how I knew this, but I did.

Following a near-death experience in the military, I became intent on seeing if it was possible to gain an understanding that would somehow end my mental turmoil and confusion. I was also set on knowing the Truth, which didn't look promising, as all I had known until then was certainly in question. I also burned to be "enlightened", although I didn't really know what that meant. I read all of the Eastern spiritual and philosophical books I could find. One day, while reading a book of Zen poetry that I had happened upon, I read the first line of what I would later discover was a famous poem, and the world fell away. I was in a space that was far beyond anything I had ever known. This was totally unexpected. I did not do drugs and had never heard of anything like this, and so was totally unprepared. Consequently, after something like an hour, the state passed. I was, however, left with a burning desire to return to whatever it was that had been there. As this had been a Zen book, I went intensely into Zen meditation. I then took up various yoga practices, at first so that I could sit longer and then later to work with the body and breath.

After finishing graduate school, I became a scientist at a national research laboratory, and then subsequently worked for over 20 years in a series of jobs in different industrial companies. To my great surprise, I eventually reached the level of a Senior Vice President in a large company and oversaw about 1000 employees and a $260MM budget.

Whenever possible, I studied with different yoga and Zen teachers and Eastern philosophers and took workshops and teachers' training courses. As I had a family, the only real free time that was normally available for practice was early in the morning. I would normally get up several hours before work to meditate and do yoga. I would also meditate in the evenings and read spiritual books when I got the chance. Several times I taught yoga and meditation courses, but ultimately stopped because I knew that I really didn't know the truth of spiritual practice.

My children were raised, went off to college, we moved many times, etc. There were many spiritual experiences, but nothing that was lasting or that ended the turmoil and confusion of my thoughts.

Somehow, I happened upon the teachings of Ramana Maharshi. I began looking in the other direction, back inside at what it was that was doing all of these practices and causing all of this confusion. One day, realizing that enlightenment was impossible as long as there was an "I" insisting on being present for the exciting conclusion as well as keeping all of its attachments, I surrendered completely. Everything was surrendered, everything; my "self", possessions, job, corner office, parking space, options, house, attachments, everything. I said deeply and sincerely from the bottom of my being, that I had to know the Truth, even if it cost my life. With that surrender, I could feel something shift.

Shortly afterwards, doing an asana that had been done thousands of times before, the "I" blew out like a candle in the wind, and a page turned. I went into the asana one way and came out transformed. Consciousness shifted completely and irrevocably. Thought stopped as a continuous activity and stillness and presence were there at a level that could never have been imagined. I realized that I was not this body, nor these thoughts, but the undying consciousness behind them. I saw that everything was perfect just as it was and that everything was somehow inside me and was in fact, all One. Surprisingly, I also realized that everything was God.

Months later, the opportunity presented itself for some extended spiritual work. I did many silent retreats and visited Zen and yoga teachers in the U.S. and India to clarify and deepen this understanding. Some time later, I found myself in another complex, high-responsibility executive position in academia where I had little training or experience and was successful, even without an "I" doing things.

For several years, although others tried to convince me to begin teaching, I resisted as it just didn't make any sense. Everyone and everything was me and it made no sense to teach an imaginary me what it already knew. There was no teacher and no one to teach. Finally, at the urging of fellow travelers, yoga teachers, and a Zen master, teaching began again. What is taught comes from nowhere just as it arises (which makes class preparation really easy). It is a mystery how and why it all happens, a mystery.

References

1. Ramana Maharshi, *Talks with Ramana Maharshi: On Realizing Abiding Peace and Happiness*, Inner Directions Publishing, Carlsbad, CA, 2000, 95—96.

2. Poonja, H.W.L., *Wake Up and Roar*, Volume I, Pacific Center Publishing, Kula, HI, 1992, 149.

3. Harrison, Steven, *Doing Nothing: Coming to the End of the Spiritual Search*, Penguin Putnam Inc., New York, NY, 1997, 3-4.

4. Parsons, Tony, *As It Is: The Open Secret to Living an Awakened Life*, Inner Directions Publishing, Carlsbad, CA, 1995-2000, 7-8.

5. Ramana Maharshi, *Talks with Ramana Maharshi: On Realizing Abiding Peace and Happiness*, Inner Directions Publishing, Carlsbad, CA, 2000, 301.

6. Swami Venkatesananda, *Enlightened Living: A New Interpretative Translation of the Yoga Sutra of Maharsi Patanjali*, Anahata Press, Sebastapol, CA, 1999, 1.

7. Osborne, Arthur, *Ramana Maharshi and the Path of Self Knowledge*, B.I. Publications, New Delhi, India, 1979, 94-95.

8. Ramana Maharshi, *Who Am I?: The Teachings of Bhagavan Sri Ramana Maharshi*, Sri Ramanasramam, Tiruvannamalai, India, 18th Edition, 2002, 8.

9. Ramana Maharshi, *Who Am I?: The Teachings of Bhagavan Sri Ramana Maharshi*, Sri Ramanasramam, Tiruvannamalai, India, 18th Edition, 2002, 13.

10. Godman, David, *Living by the Words of Bhagavan*, Sri Annamalai Swami Ashram Trust, Tiruvannamalai, India, 1994, 299.

11. Masterpasqua, F., and Perna, P., *The Psychological Meaning of Chaos: Translating Theory into Practice*, American Psychological Association, Washington, DC, 1997, 36-37.

12. Ramana Maharshi, *Talks with Ramana Maharshi: On Realizing Abiding Peace and Happiness*, Inner Directions Publishing, Carlsbad, CA, 2000, 110.

13. Ramana Maharshi, *Who Am I?: The Teachings of Bhagavan Sri Ramana Maharshi,* Sri Ramanasramam, Tiruvannamalai, India, 18th Edition, 2002, 10.

14. Kapleau, Roshi Philip, *The Three Pillars of Zen: Teaching, Practice and Enlightenment*, Anchor Press, Garden City, NY, 1980, 281-304.

15. World Book Encyclopedia, *Aquinas, St. Thomas,* Field Enterprises Educational Corporation, Chicago, IL, 1971, 543.

16. Ramana Maharshi, *Talks with Ramana Maharshi: On Realizing Abiding Peace and Happiness*, Inner Directions Publishing, Carlsbad, CA, 2000, 186.

17. Ramana Maharshi, *Talks with Ramana Maharshi: On Realizing Abiding Peace and Happiness*, Inner Directions Publishing, Carlsbad, CA, 2000, 418.

Bibliography

Adams, Robert, *Silence of the Heart: Dialogues with Robert Adams*, Acropolis Books, Atlanta, GA, 1999.

Adyashanti, *The Impact of Awakening*, Open Gate Publishing, Los Gatos, CA, 2000.

Begley, Sharon, *Train Your Mind, Change Your Brain*, Ballantine Books, New York, NY, 2007.

Csikszentmihalyi, Mihaly, *Flow: The Psychology of Optimal Experience*, Harper and Row, New York, NY, 1990.

Dayananda Saraswati, Swami, *Bhagavadgita Home Study Program*, Arsha Vidya Gurukulam, Saylorsburg, PA, 1989.

Dayananda Saraswati, Swami, *Talks on Upadesa Saram (Essence of the Teaching) of Ramana Maharshi*, Sri Gangadhareswar Trust, Rishikesh, India, 1987.

Deutsch, Eliot, *The Bhagavad Gita*, Holt, Rinehart and Winston, NY, NY, 1968. Tolle, Eckhardt *The Power of Now: A Guide to Spiritual Fulfillment*, New World Library, Novato, CA, 1999.

Gleick, James, *Chaos: Making a New Science*, Viking Penguin Press, New York, NY, 1987.

Godman, David, *Living by the Words of Bhagavan*, Sri Annamalai Swami Ashram Trust, Tiruvannamalai, India, 1994.

Godman, David, *Papaji: Interviews*, Avadhuta Foundation, Boulder, CO, 1993, 35.

Goleman, Daniel, *Destructive Emotions: A Scientific Dialogue with the Dalai Lama*, Bantam Dell, New York, NY, 2003.

Harrison, Steven, *Doing Nothing: Coming to the End of the Spiritual Search*, Penguin Putnam, NY, NY, 1998.

Hixon, Lex, *Great Swan: Meetings with Ramakrishna*, Larson Publications, Burdett, NY, 1996.

Johari, Harish, *Chakras: Energy Centers of Transformation*, Destiny Books, Rochester, VT, 1987.

Kaas, J.H. "Why Is Brain Size So Important: Design Problems and Solutions as Neocortex Get Bigger or Smaller", *Brain and Mind*, 1:2000.

Kapleau, Philip, *The Three Pillars of Zen: Teaching, Practice and Enlightenment*, Anchor Books, Garden City, NY, 1980.

Katie, Byron, *Loving What Is: Four Questions That Can Change Your Life*, Three Rivers Press, New York, NY, 2002.

Kaushik, R. P., *Organic Alchemy*, Journey Publications, Woodstock, NY, 1978.

Kraftsow, Gary, *Nirvana Shatakam: Sri Sankaracarya Krtam*, unpublished manuscript, Haiku, HI, 1999.

Kraftsow, Gary, *Yoga for Wellness: Healing with the Timeless Teachings of Viniyoga*, Penguin Arkana, New York, NY, 1999.

Kraftsow, Gary, *Yoga for Transformation: Ancient Teachings and Practices for Healing the Body, Mind and Heart*, Penguin Compass, New York, NY, 2002.

Krishnamoorthi Aiyer, N. R., *The Essence of Ribhu Gita*, Sri Ramanasramam, Tiruvannamalai, India, 1984.

Krishnamurti, J., *Krishnamurti's Notebook*, Harper and Row, NY, NY, 1976.

Krishnamurti, J., *The Awakening of Intelligence*, Harper and Row, San Francisco, CA, 1973.

Kundert-Gibbs, John L., *No-thing Is Left To Tell: Zen and Chaos Theory in the Dramatic Art of Samuel Beckett*, Associated University Presses, Cranbury, NJ, 1999.

Libet, Benjamin, *Mind Time: The Temporal Factor in Consciousness*, Harvard University Press, Cambridge, MA, 2004.

Masterpasqua, F., and Perna, P., *The Psychological Meaning of Chaos: Translating Theory into Practice*, American Psychological Association, Washington, DC, 1997.

Miller, Richard, *The Breath of Life*, Sebastopol, CA.

Mitchell, Stephen, *Bhagavad Gita*, Three Rivers Press, New York, NY, 2000.
Narasimhaswami, B. V., *Upadesa Saram or Upadesa Undiyar of Ramana Maharshi*, Sri Ramanasramam, Tiruvannamalai, India, 1980.

Natarajan, A.R. and Viswanatha Swami, *Upadesa Saram (Essence of Teaching)*, Ramana Maharshi Centre for Learning, Bangalore, India, 1997.

Nhat Hanh, Thich, *The Miracle of Mindfulness: A Manual on Meditation*, Beacon Press, Boston, MA, 1976.

Nisargadatta Maharaj, *I Am That: Talks with Sri Nisargadatta Maharaj*, The Acorn Press, Durham, NC, 1973.

Parsons, Tony, *As It Is: The Open Secret to Living an Awakened Life*, Inner Directions, Carlsbad, CA, 1995.

Parsons, Tony, *Invitation to Awaken: Embracing Our Natural State of Presence*, Inner Directions, Carlsbad, CA, 2004.

Paul, Russill, *The Yoga of Sound: Tapping the Hidden Power of Music and Chant*, New World Library, Novato, CA, 2006.

Pierce, Margaret D. and Martin G., *Yoga for Your Life: A Practice Manual of Breath and Movement for Every Body*, Rudra Press, Portland, OR, 1996.

Ram Dass and Levine, Steven, *Grist for the Mill*, Unity Press, Santa Cruz, CA, 1976.

Ramana Maharshi, *Talks with Ramana Maharshi: On Realizing Abiding Peace and Happiness,* Inner Directions Publishing, Carlsbad, CA, 2000.

Ramana Maharshi, *The Song Celestial,* Sri Ramanasramam, Tiruvannamalai, India, 1995.

Ramana Maharshi, *Who Am I?: The Teachings of Ramana Maharshi,* Sri Ramanasramam, Tiruvannamalai, India, 2001.

Reps, Paul, *Zen Flesh, Zen Bones: A Collection of Zen and Pre-Zen Writings,* Charles E. Tuttle, Rutland, VT, 1957.

Savin, Olga, *The Way of a Pilgrim And A Pilgrim Continues On His Way,* Shambhala Publications, Boston, MA, 2001.

Segal, Suzanne, *Collision with the Infinite: A Life Beyond the Personal Self,* Blue Dove Press, San Diego, CA, 1996.

Shimano, Eido Roshi, *Daily Sutras for Chanting and Recitation,* The Zen Studies Society, NY, NY, 1982.

Sivananda, Swami, *The Bhagavad Gita,* The Divine Life Society, Shivanandanagar, U.P., India, 1995.

Steig, William, *Strutters & Fretters or The Inescapable Self,* Harper Collins, NY, NY, 1992.

Tejomayanandji, Swami, *Sree Shankaracharya's Nirvana Shatakam,* Central Chinmaya Mission Trust, Bombay, India, 1988.

Venkatesananda, Swami, *Enlightened Living: A New Interpretative Translation of the Yoga Sutras of Maharshi Patanjali, Anahata Press,* Sebastapol, CA, 1999.

Viditatmananda, Swami, *Upadesa Saram with Swami Viditatmananda: Vedanta Retreat Tapes and Notes,* Arsha Vidya Gurukulam, Saylorsburg, PA, 1999.

Vishnudevananda, Swami, *The Complete Illustrated Book of Yoga,* Bell Publishing, NY, NY, 1960.

Woodroffe, John Sir, *The Serpent Power,* Ganesh and Co., Madras, India, 1973.

Other Useful Sources for Further Work

Barks, Coleman, and Green, Michael, *The Illuminated Rumi*, Broadway Books, NY, NY, 1997.

Desikachar, T.K.V., *The Heart of Yoga: Developing a Personal Practice*, Inner Traditions International, Rochester, VT, 1995.

Harding, Douglas, *Look for Yourself: The Science and Art of Self Realization*, Inner Directions Publishing, Encinitas, CA, 1998.

Jean Klein, *Who Am I?: The Sacred Quest*, Element Books Ltd., Dorset, UK, 1988.

Lok To, *The Prajna Paramita Heart Sutra*, The Corporate Body of the Buddha Educational Foundation, Taipei, Taiwan, 1998.

Mohan, A. G., *Yoga for Body, Breath, and Mind: A Guide to Personal Reintegration*, Rudra Press, Portland, OR, 1993.

Osho, *The Book of Secrets*, St. Martin's Griffin, NY, 1974.

Packer, Toni, *Seeing Without Knowing: Writings on Zen Work*, Genesee Valley Zen Center, Springwater, NY, 1983.

Packer, Toni, *The Work of This Moment: Awareness in Daily Life*, Springwater Center, Springwater, NY, 1988.

978-0-595-41856-5
0-595-41856-2